Northeast of Eden

ATLAS OF MORMON SETTLEMENT IN CALDWELL COUNTY, MISSOURI, 1834–39

John C. Hamer

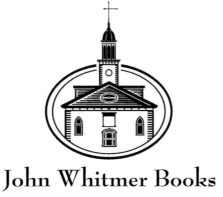

John Whitmer Books

Independence, Missouri

2011

Northeast of Eden: Atlas of Mormon Settlement in Caldwell County, Missouri, 1834–39
By John C. Hamer

Published by John Whitmer Books
Independence, Missouri
JohnWhitmerBooks.com

Printed in the United States of America

ISBN-13 978-1-934901-07-6

Acknowledgments — I would like to thank Ronald Romig for his assistance and encouragement with this map project and I would also like to credit Steven LeSueur, Alexander Baugh, Mel Tungate and Michael Riggs for making many helpful suggestions and corrections to the maps. Work on the land records database would have been impossible without the assistance of Michael Karpowicz, whom I would also like to acknowledge and credit.

Cover and interior design, illustration, cartography, and typesetting by John C. Hamer.

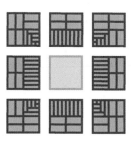

Introduction

IN THE COURSE of their many migrations, 19th century Mormons left their mark on a number of landscapes across the North American continent. The remains are still apparent in some of these locales: the spacious temple in Kirtland, Ohio, is an impressive monument that speaks to the vision and ambition of the early Latter Day Saints who gathered there. Likewise, the many well-built brick homes and shops that survive in Nauvoo speak to the industry of the Mormons who built their own city-state on the Mississippi.

Much less remains to mark the Mormon presence in Caldwell County, Missouri, where the early Latter Day Saint church had its headquarters between the Kirtland and Nauvoo periods. Only one structure survives from the Mormon period: a dilapidated log house, originally belonging to Charles C. Rich, an early church member who went on to become an apostle under Brigham Young.[1] All that remains in the former county seat, the one-time Mormon headquarters town of Far West, are the cornerstones of the never-finished temple. All other relics of the town — the roads, the buildings, even the graves in the burying ground — have reverted to farmland.

Beyond these scant remains, the main visible imprint on the landscape surviving from the Mormon period is the survey of the county itself. The maps in this atlas attempt to identify that imprint by applying information from Mormon-period land records to the terrain as it exists today.

---

[1] See "Caldwell County, Missouri, Log House on Charles C. Rich Property Update," *Missouri Mormon Frontier Foundation Newsletter,* no. 11 (Summer 1996): 4–5; and "The Rich-Wallace-Gardner Log House," *Missouri Mormon Frontier Foundation Newsletter,* no. 14 (Summer 1997): 8–9.

MAP 1: Kirtland, Ohio, and Indpendence, Missouri — the two centers of Mormonism in the early 1830s — were nearly on opposite sides of the country. Just beyond Missouri's western frontier was the unorganized territory into which the U.S. federal government was relocating Indians native to the eastern states.

Background History

MORMON ACTIVITY IN Missouri began soon after the church was organized in April of 1830. In the fall of that year, the church's second elder, Oliver Cowdery, led a mission to share the newly revealed gospel of the Book of Mormon with American Indians.[2] At the time, it was U.S. policy to relocate Indian tribes from the East onto the Great Plains. The government settled the Indians beyond the western border of Missouri, which was planned as a permanent Indian frontier line. The final stop before reaching Indian Territory was the boom-town of Independence, in Jackson County, Missouri.[3] Cowdery and his companions had little luck converting Indians to Mormonism, but the mission impressed the Mormon prophet Joseph Smith with Independence's strategic lo-

---

[2] Cowdery was called by revelation in September of 1830 to lead a mission to the "Lamanites" — the Book of Mormon term for American Indians, see Phillip R. Legg, *Oliver Cowdery: The Elusive Second Elder of the Restoration*, 50-53. The revelation is recorded in the Book of Commandments (1833) XXX:7-16, D&C (1835) LI:3-5, D&C (Missouri, 2000) 27:3a–5c, D&C (Utah, 2000) 28:8–16.

[3] The town of Independence was a mere 12 miles east of the state line, Max H. Parkin, "Independence, Missouri," in *The Atlas of Mormonism*, 40

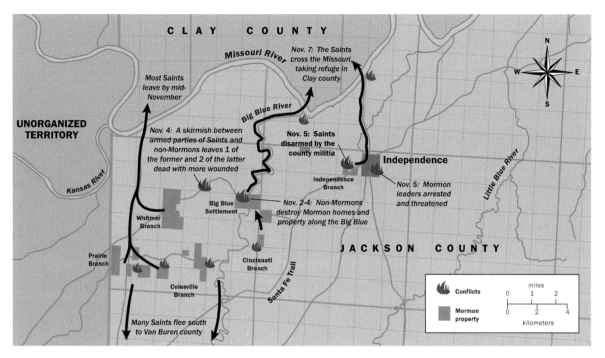

MAP 2: Conflict between the Mormons and their neighbors led to the expulsion of nearly all of the latter from Jackson County, Missouri, in 1833. The Missouri Saints took refuge in neighboring counties.

cation. In a revelation given in Missouri in July of 1831, Smith taught that Independence would become the "center place" for the city of Zion, the New Jerusalem, when Christ returned again to the Earth.[4]

The revelation and the accompanying commandment to gather had the effect of encouraging early Latter Day Saints to move to Independence and the surrounding area in Jackson County in preparation for the imminent Second Coming. Mormon settlement in the area was rapid — perhaps 800 had moved to the county by the end of 1832, swelling to 1,200 by the summer of 1833.[5] Church headquarters and the prophet himself remained in the East, in Kirtland, Ohio, which also saw its Mormon population swell rapidly. Nine hundred miles and irregular communication separated these two primary nuclei of Mormon settlement in the 1830s (see map 1).[6] Mormons and their neighbors did not get along well in either location, but the opposition the Saints met in Jackson County was much more determined and fierce. By the end of 1833, organized vigilante groups

---

[4] D&C (1835) XXVII:1, D&C (Missouri) 57:1a–g, D&C (Utah) 57:1–5.

[5] Richard H. Jackson, "First Gathering to Zion," in *Historical Atlas of Mormonism,* 34.

[6] Bruce A. Van Orden, "From Kirtland to Missouri," in *Historical Atlas of Mormonism,* 26.

in Jackson County succeeded in expelling most of the Mormon settlers, who were forced to take refuge in neighboring counties (see map 2). Clay County, in particular, housed most of the Mormons as they sought various means of returning to their land in Jackson County.[7] The Missourians in Jackson County, however, remained firm in their opposition and as years elapsed with no progress, the Missourians in Clay County began to push for a permanent solution to the "Mormon problem."[8] This they achieved in 1836, when the Missouri legislature created a new county, set aside specifically for Mormon settlement. This new Mormon county, to the northeast of Clay County, was named Caldwell (see maps 3a and 3b).[9]

Although leaders at church headquarters in Kirtland held out hope for the "redemption of Zion" (a return to Mormon lands in Jackson County), the weary leadership of the church in Missouri embraced the compromise and began the work of relocating the Missouri Saints to Caldwell County, even before the county was formally created. Land throughout the county was surveyed and made ready for agriculture. Thousands of acres of land were purchased from the Federal government by individual Mormons and also by the local church leadership on behalf of the church. In the western portion of the county, Missouri church leaders John Whitmer and W.W. Phelps laid out a 1 square mile plat (later expanded to 4 square miles) for a town which they named Far West. Far West became the county seat and the settlement grew very quickly (see map 4).

While the Saints began to settle in and build up Caldwell County, the church in Kirtland began to unravel. Finally, in the spring of 1838, Joseph Smith and his chief counselor, Sidney Rigdon, abandoned Ohio permanently and relocated with their families to Far West. With them came hundreds of loyalists from Kirtand and the pace of Mormon settlement in northwestern Missouri quickened still further. Far West became the headquarters of the Latter Day Saint church, which was now renamed, the "Church of Jesus Christ of Latter Day Saints."[10] In the process of relocating the headquarters, supporters

---

[7] Ibid.

[8] Alexander Doniphan, a non-Mormon member of the Missouri legislature from Clay County, made the proposal for the creation of a special Mormon county. Stephen C. LeSueur, *The 1838 Mormon War in Missouri*, 23–25.

[9] Clark V. Johnson, "Northern Missouri," in *Historical Atlas of Mormonism*, 42.

[10] The variant punctuations "Latter Day Saints" and "Latter-day Saints" were not standardized until after the Mormon succession crisis of 1844. Today, the usage "Latter Day Saints" refers to the whole movement, while "Latter-day Saints" refers solely to members of The Church of Jesus Christ of Latter-day Saints head-

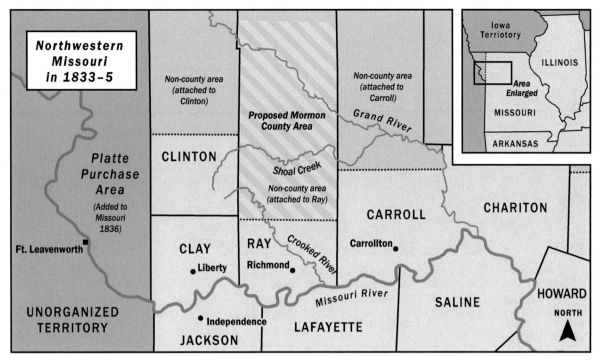

MAP 3A: Northwestern Missouri was still being organized in the 1830s. When it became clear that the Mormons could not return to their homes in Jackson County, a proposed compromise envisioned organizing a new county north of Ray County, specifically for Mormon settlement.

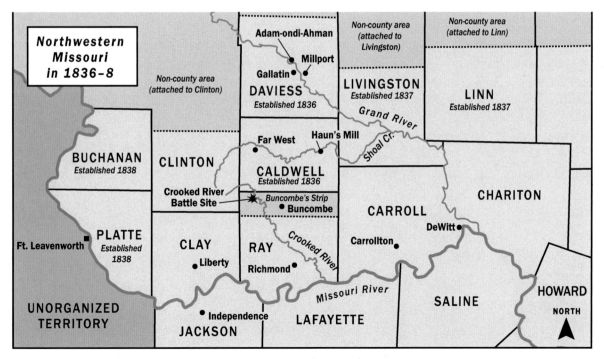

MAP 3B: The Mormon county of Caldwell, was smaller than envisioned and it was hemmed in on the north by the newly created Daviess County.

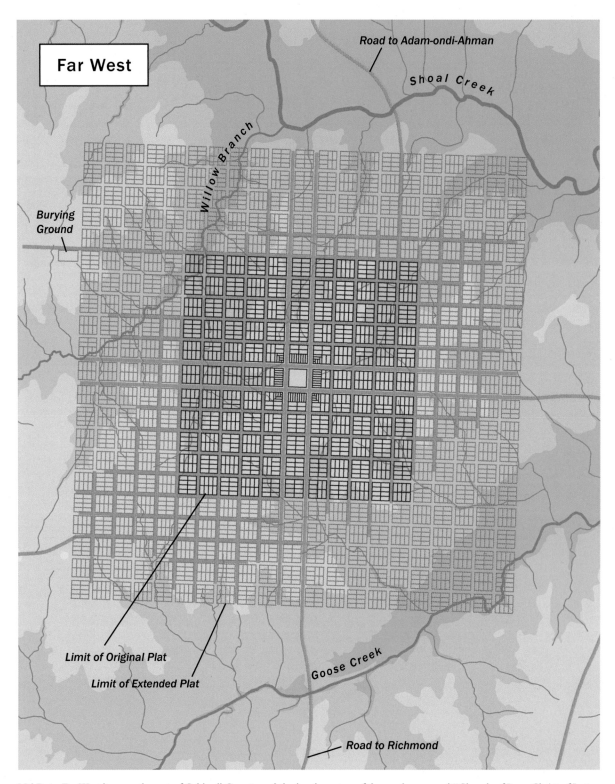

MAP 4: Far West became the seat of Caldwell County and the headquarters of the newly renamed "Church of Jesus Christ of Latter Day Saints." Its original one square mile plat of Far West was expanded to encompass four square miles.

of the general church presidency — Joseph Smith, Sidney Rigdon, and Joseph's brother Hyrum — came into conflict with the Missouri church leaders including Oliver Cowdery, John and David Whitmer, and W.W. Phelps. In the resulting power struggle, the Missouri leadership and their loyalists were excommunicated or withdrew from church fellowship and as a group they became known as "dissenters."[11]

Meanwhile, as Mormon immigration to the region increased, Church leaders began to plant new Mormon settlements in the counties surrounding Caldwell.[12] Daviess County and the non-county territory separating Ray and Caldwell Counties (known as Buncombe's Strip), in particular, were heavily settled by Mormons. Mormons also purchased the settlement of DeWitt in Carroll County, near the confluence of the Missouri and Grand Rivers. This expansion renewed the fears of non-Mormons in northwestern Missouri that Mormons would one day out-number them and that non-Mormons would lose political and economic control of the whole area to the church. The climate of fear allowed more radical non-Mormons to take the lead and organize opposition to Mormon settlement in general. Perceived threats from non-Mormons living in surrounding counties and from the dissenters living in Caldwell County, coupled with the fresh example of the Kirtland failures, led Joseph Smith, Sidney Rigdon, and other church leaders to adopt a militant posture. An auxiliary known as the Danites was organized that quickly succeeded in expelling most of the vocal dissenters and their families from Caldwell County.[13] The leadership also organized a regular militia, which paraded alongside the Danites in a 4th of July celebration. Addressing the assembly that day, Rigdon announced that if any "mob" attacked the Mormons, "it shall be between us and them a war of extermination; for we will follow them, 'til the last drop of their blood is spilled..."[14]

A series of escalating conflicts between Mormons and Missourians followed (see map 5), during which the governor of Missouri called out 2,500 state militiamen[15] and issued

quartered in Salt Lake City, Utah. See Newell G. Bringhurst and John C. Hamer, *Scattering of the Saints: Schism within Mormonism*, 15–17,

[11] LeSueur, 37–38.

[12] Mormon settlement appears to have occurred in Carroll, Chariton, Livingston, Clinton, Randolph, Monroe, Lafayette, Ray and Daviess Counties. See Clark V. Johnson, *Mormon Redress Petitions: Documents of the 1833-38 Missouri Conflict*, p. xxix, and also LeSueur, 30–31.

[13] LeSueur, 37–47.

[14] Ibid., 50.

[15] Alexander L. Baugh, *A Call to Arms: The 1838 Mormon Defense of Northern Missouri*, 109.

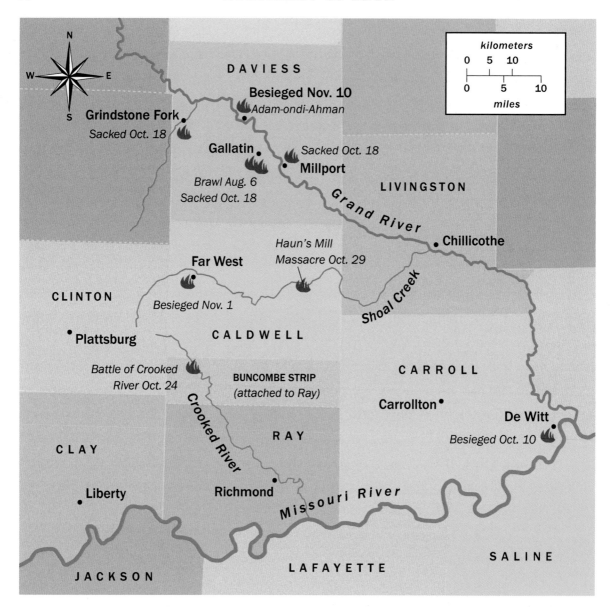

MAP 5: Points of conflict in the 1838 Mormon Missouri War.

his famous order, that the "Mormons must be treated as enemies, and must be exterminated or driven from the State if necessary, for the public peace..."[16] In the face of overwhelming odds, as state militia surrounded Far West at the end of October, 1838, Smith, Rigdon and other church leaders surrendered and gave themselves up for trial.[17] The illegal terms imposed by the Missouri militia commander obliged every Mormon to

[16] LeSueur., 152.

[17] Ibid., 168.

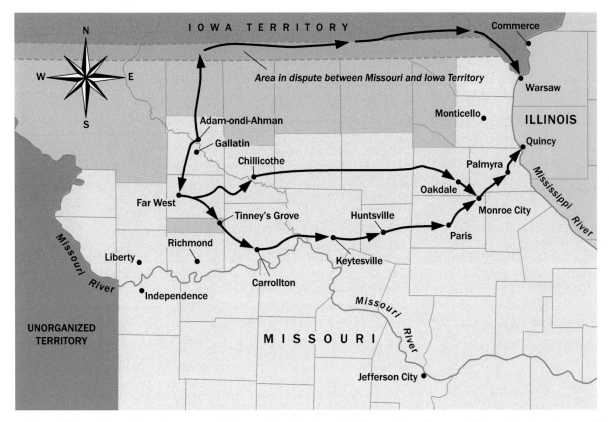

MAP 6: The majority of the Mormon population was forced to leave their homes in northwestern Missouri by the early part of 1839. A few left the state the quickest way possible, north to the Iowa territory and then east to Illinois. Most traveled east in two general routes along established roads. The northern route passed through Chillicothe and the southern through Tinney's Grove and Keytesville. The Saints regrouped in Quincy, Illinois, where many citizens responded to their plight by opening their homes to the refugees.

leave the state and to sign over their lands to pay for the militia muster.[18] In early 1839, the bulk of the Saints left Missouri, taking refuge in Illinois (see map 6). As a result, Caldwell County's population — which reached between 5,000 and 7,000 at its height — was reduced to less than 1,000.[19] A century and a half later, nearly all that has survived

---

[18] Ibid., 180–194.

[19] Because the bulk of the Mormon population settled the county so briefly, and because no census was conducted during their stay, population estimates vary. Stephen LeSueur puts the Mormon population of Caldwell at "about 5,000," LeSueur, 36. Clark V. Johnson and Ronald E. Romig put Caldwell's population at "more than 7,000" in *An Index to Early Caldwell County, Missouri Land Records*, vii. LaMar C. Berrett estimates Caldwell's population was "about 10,000" inhabitants in *Sacred Places: Missouri: A Comprehensive Guide to Early LDS Historical Sites* (Salt Lake City: Deseret Book, 2004), 289. This inflated figure includes a population estimate of "5,000" for the town Far West alone. According to Johnson and Romig, vi, Far West had perhaps 150 crude log homes at its height. A population of 5,000 would demand at least 33 residents per home.

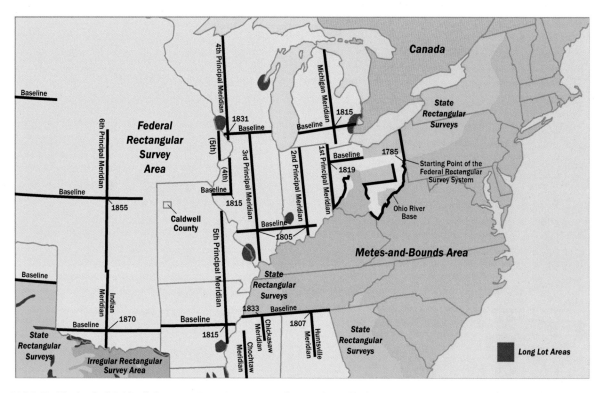

MAP 7: The land of Caldwell County, Missouri was surveyed using the Federal Rectangular system. Its 12 statute townships were measured north and west of the 5th Principal Meridian and Baseline. (The dates indicate the initiation of the survey of each meridian and baseline.)

in the county to mark the Mormon presence is a single log house and, of course, the land itself.

The Land Records

T HE LANDS OF Caldwell County are part of the great American grid that began with the Land Ordinance of 1785. Previously, most land in America had been parceled off in irregular shapes using "metes and bounds." In this system, the survey began with a recognized landmark and then followed a compass line or a waterway to another identified point and so on until the property was completely bounded. However, since the points in question were often such landmarks as "a very large rock" or "a great stump," the system resulted in endless confusion and litigation.[20]

The rectangular survey greatly simplified property titles by imposing a standardized grid on the landscape. The Federal government began the survey of each region

---

[20] *Historical Atlas of the United States,* 98.

opened up for settlement by marking off an east-west running baseline and a principal meridian running north and south. From these reference lines, land was divided into statute townships, 6 miles wide by 6 miles tall. Each statute township was identified by a township number north or south of the baseline, and a range number east or west of the principal meridian. Caldwell County was composed of 12 of these statute townships — Townships 55 thru 57 north, and Ranges 26 thru 29 west of the 5th Principal Meridian.[21] Each statute township across the country was further divided into 36 numbered sections, each 1 mile square. The Land Ordinance specified that lands in section 16 of each township would be sold for the benefit local schools. Land in the remaining sections was divided into parcels of a full section (640 acres), a half section (320 acres), a quarter section (160 acres), a half quarter section (80 acres) or a quarter quarter section (40 acres).[22]

The twelve townships that eventually became Caldwell County were first surveyed and recorded in 1824-25.

[21] Johnson and Romig, 1-12.

[22] For a helpful description of the Land Ordinance system, see *Historical Atlas of the United States*, 98–99.

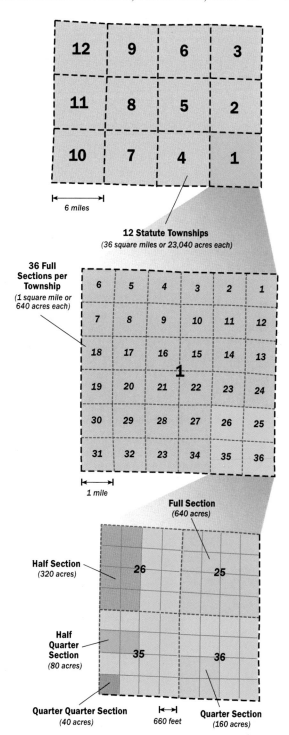

MAP 8: Caldwell County is made up of 12 Statute Townships, 6 miles on each side, numbered north and west of the 5th Principal Meridian. Each of these townships is divided into 36 Sections of 1 square mile each. Each Section was further divided into Half Sections, Quarter Sections, Half Quarter Sections and Quarter Sections.

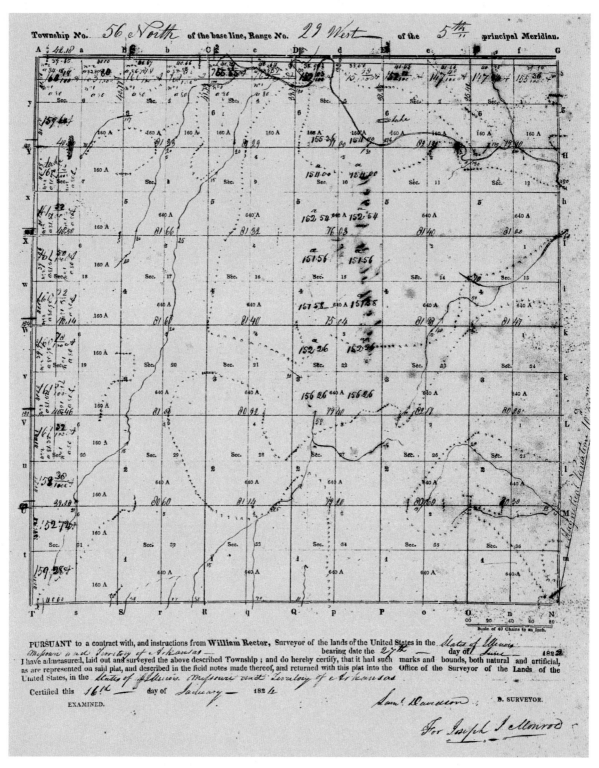

MAP 9: The original 1824 survey of Township 56 North of the baseline and 29 West of the 5th Principal Meridian, what today is Mirabile Township (township #11) in Caldwell County. The survey divides the township into sections and quarter sections and marks out the streams and also the division between prairielands and timber lands.

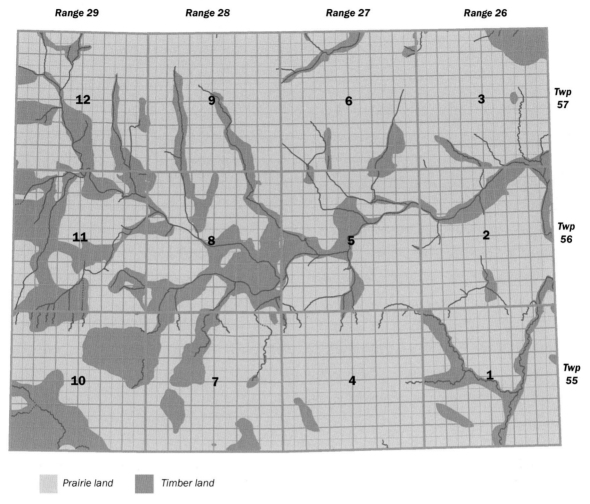

Range 29   Range 28   Range 27   Range 26

MAP 10: A composite of the original survey maps, showing the twelve townships of Caldwell County, divided into sections and quarter sections, highlighting the creeks, prairie land, and timber land.

The original survey plats or, in some cases, direct copies of the originals have survived, giving us a reasonable picture of the terrain as it existed immediately prior to settlement. The survey plats show the divisions of each township into sections and quarter sections. In addition, they record the path of creeks and the division of between prairie lands and timber lands (see map 9). Timber lands were especially prized even though they needed to be cleared prior to farming. The cut wood provided both building material homes as well as fuel to heat them. In addition, settlers from the eastern U.S. were unfamiliar with hard prairie turf, which they were ill-equipped to plow and which they (incorrectly) believed was less fertile than the timber lands. A composite of all the original surveys shows that townships that became Caldwell County had a good mix between wooded and un-wooded lands (see map 10).

Property in these twelve townships began to be sold as early as 1829 out of the regional government land office in Lexington, Missouri (about 25 miles south of Caldwell County). These lands were auctioned at a minimum price of $1.25 per acre, and rarely sold for more than the minimum price. A purchaser could also pay the surveyor's fee to enter the track with the government and then complete the purchase by paying the balance owed within two or three years.[23]

Although small number of non-Mormon settlers began to purchase land in what would become Caldwell County as early as 1829, less than 4,000 acres of land had been purchased in the 12 townships as of 1835. The amount of land purchased increased dramatically in 1836, as the Saints moved to the area in response to the plan to create a Mormon county. Mormons bought even more land in 1837. By 1839, when most of the Mormons were forced to leave the state, over 50,000 acres of land in Caldwell County had been purchased from the Federal government (see map 11). Although the early county records themselves perished in a tragic fire in 1860, the Federal government retained records of the initial purchases of land. The name of the original owner and the date of purchase were recorded onto a series of 12 plat maps that are now housed in the Caldwell County Recorder's Office. [24] Clark V. Johnson and Ron Romig used these plat maps to create an index of the land records which was published by the Missouri Mormon Frontier Foundation. Although the records do not include the purchase price, resale information, or subsequent subdivisions of the land and although they cannot show land settlers squatted on without purchasing — they are nonetheless valuable for the snapshot that they do provide.

Mapping Caldwell County

THIS ATLAS PRIMARILY consists of a series forty-eight maps that combines and compares the original 1824 survey plats, the land records from the Mormon period (property sold by the Federal government 1829-39), and modern terrain information from the U.S. Geological Survey (USGS). The base level of each map is derived from

<hr>

[23] Johnson and Romig, iii.

[24] Ibid., iii–iv.

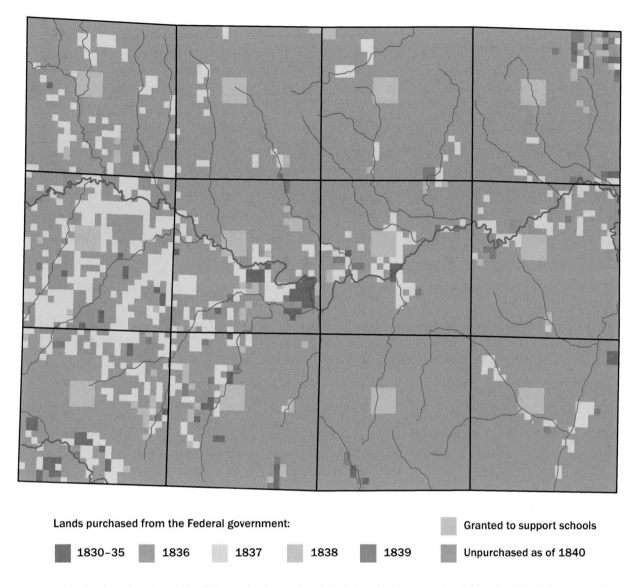

Lands purchased from the Federal government:

■ 1830–35	■ 1836	■ 1837	■ 1838	■ 1839	

■ Granted to support schools

■ Unpurchased as of 1840

MAP 11: Land Purchased in Caldwell County by date. Relatively little land had been purchased from the Federal Government in the 1830-1835 period, prior to heavy Mormon settlement in the area. This changed in 1836 and 1837 as Mormons gathered to the new county and began to bring the woods and prairies into agricultural production.

USGS topographical maps published in 1984. This level provides us with the section lines, the current terrain elevation, the modern course of creeks, as well as modern roads for reference. The next layer is drawn from the original survey plats, which indicate the location of the more desirable timber lands and the less desirable prairie lands at the time of the original settlement. Because the survey plats and the USGS topo maps show creeks, it is possible to compare changes in their courses between 1824 and 1984. Unfortunately, the 1824 plats are significantly less detailed and accurate than the 1984 topo maps, and we cannot say with confidence whether a creek has, in fact, moved, or whether the original survey was simply inaccurate. The final map layer lists the first purchaser of each patent and the date of purchase as recorded in the land records. The map series follows on pages XX through XX of this atlas.

Several immediate observations can be drawn from this new series of maps. Most obvious is that early settlement followed the creek beds. This confirms hints left to us in narrative sources, but the pattern on the ground is somewhat different than prior speculation. For example, a map in the 1994 *Atlas of Mormonism* emphasized the entire length of Shoal Creek as an area of heavy settlement.[25] The new maps show us that settlement was heaviest in the westernmost townships, not only along Shoal Creek, but also along Goose Creek, Log Creek, Tub Creek, Plum Creek and Brushy Creek. A much larger proportion of the land around these creeks was purchased in the western townships relative to land bought around Shoal Creek in the eastern townships (recall map 11). When the location of timber lands and prairie lands are added, the preference for timber land is confirmed (see map 12). Nevertheless, a considerable amount of timber land, especially in the eastern portion of the county went unpurchased during the Mormon period. At the same time, large tracts of prairie land were purchased, especially around Far West. This illustrates that the county was no where close to being "filled up" during the Mormon period.

Also immediately apparent from Map 11 is the sudden, unexpected fall-off in land purchases beginning in 1838. Whereas 19,560 acres had been purchased in 1836 and 26,280 in 1837, the number drops to a mere 1,920 acres in 1838. If anything, the pace of Mormon immigration and settlement must have quickened in 1838, with the abandonment of Kirtland and the relocation of church headquarters to Far West. Although some of the 1838 immigrants were clearly being sent to settle areas outside Caldwell County, it seems unlikely that this factor alone accounts for a drop-off of more than 90%. The most likely conclusion is that while Missouri church leaders (in 1836 and 1837) had a policy of buying up the land, the general church presidency which assumed control in 1838 determined that the Saints should begin to squat on new land without paying the Federal government. Since squatters are unrecorded, the pattern of settlement in 1838 is lost.

---

[25] Clark V. Johnson, "Northern Missouri," in *Historical Atlas of Mormonism*, 42–43.

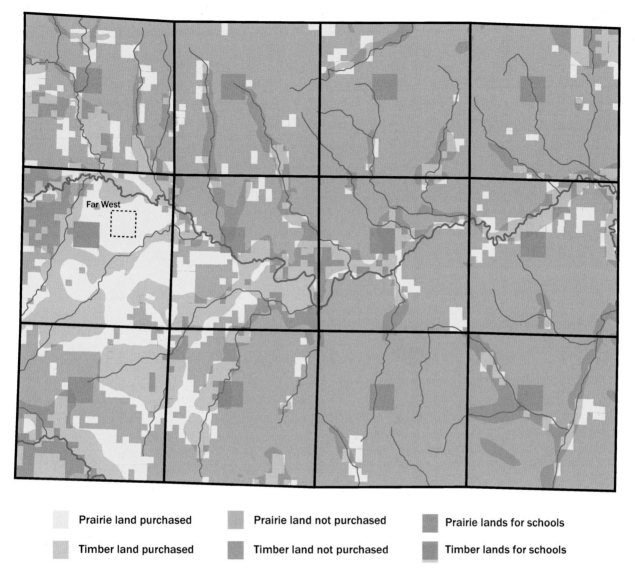

Prairie land purchased   Prairie land not purchased   Prairie lands for schools

Timber land purchased   Timber land not purchased   Timber lands for schools

MAP 12: Prairie land and timber land purchased as of 1840. Although timber land was clearly preferred, large tracts remained available during the Mormon period, especially in the eastern half of the county. Meanwhile, in the western third of the county, settlers purchased a large amount of prairie land.

Analyzed closely, the land records can also be used to map the large gulfs that separated the major purchasers from the minor purchasers of land in the Mormon period. The ten largest land-buyers accounted for 12.9% of the land bought up through 1839. The top twenty accounted for a total of 19.2% of the land purchased. Some of these top purchasers: John Whitmer (1120 acres), W.W. Phelps (1080 acres), Oliver Cowdery (640 acres), and Joseph Smith (560 acres) were clearly buying land as agents of the Church of

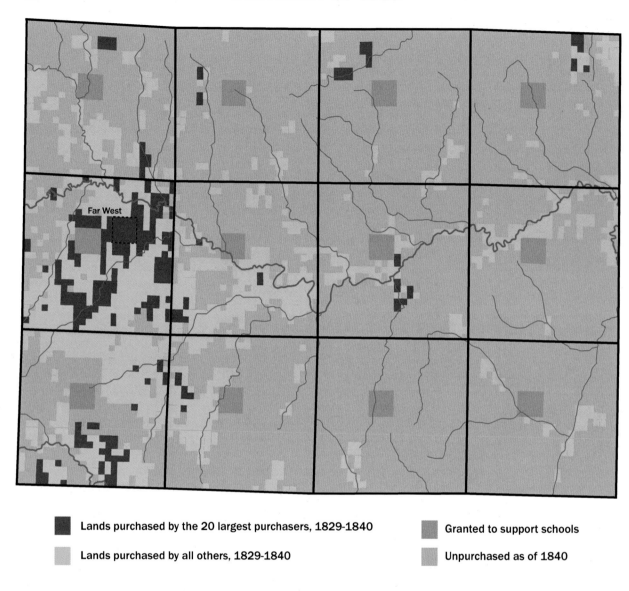

	Lands purchased by the 20 largest purchasers, 1829-1840		Granted to support schools
	Lands purchased by all others, 1829-1840		Unpurchased as of 1840

MAP 13: Lands purchased by the twenty largest land-purchasers plotted against lands purchased by all others.

the Latter Day Saints. Others, like Squire Bozorth (760 acres) and his brothers, John and Abner Bozorth (400 and 360 acres, respectively), seem to have been acting on their own initiative. In contrast to large land-owners like these, the majority of purchasers — including men like King Follet, Alpheus Cutler, George Beebe and Porter Rockwell — bought only a single quarter-quarter section, amounting to just 40 acres each (see map 13).

One surprising observation that can be drawn from the maps is that non-Mormon purchases in Caldwell County continued through the Mormon period. Despite Joseph

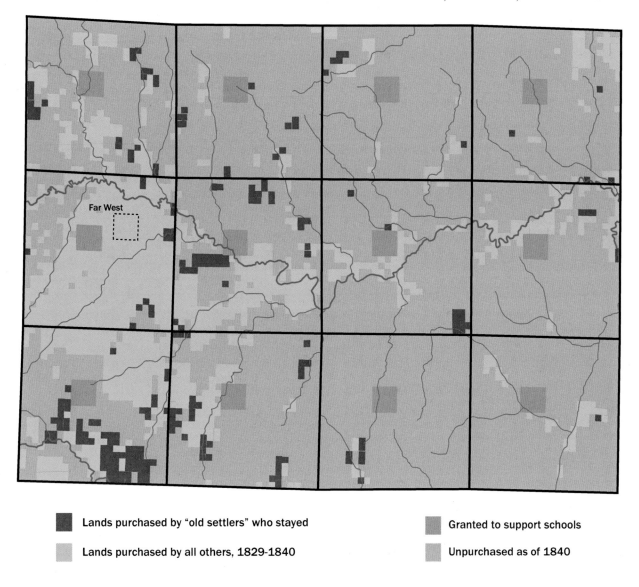

Lands purchased by "old settlers" who stayed

Granted to support schools

Lands purchased by all others, 1829-1840

Unpurchased as of 1840

MAP 14: Lands purchased by individuals who continued to make purchases before, during, and after the Mormon period.

Smith's boast that "the old settlers will sell for half price, yes, for quarter price [—] they are determined to get away,"[26] some of the old settlers were continuing to purchase land throughout the Mormon period. In fact, one of the county's earliest non-Mormon residents, Samuel K. McGee,[27] was one of the top land purchasers during the Mormon

---

[26] September 1838 letter to Stephen Post, quoted in LeSueur, 36.

[27] I am especially indebted to the work of Ronald Romig and Michael Riggs in identifying early roads both in the primary sources and on the ground today. In his 1840 redress petition, Orrin Porter Rockwell re-

Period. McGee's family came to the area in 1819 and had been among of the earliest permanent residents in Clay and Ray counties. He himself began to purchase land in the Rockford area of what became Caldwell County in 1832 and 1833. He continued to buy land there in 1836 and 1837 and was still actively buying land in the 1850s, long after the Mormons had gone. Up through 1839, McGee had purchased 720 acres of land in Caldwell County from the Federal Government, making him the largest single purchaser after Mormons John Whitmer, W.W. Phelps, Hyrum Smith, Squire Bozarth and John Daley. Other old non-Mormon residents who continued to buy land from 1836-1839 include Francis McGuire (320 acres just east of present-day Kingston), John Conner and Stephen Woolsey (320 acres and 80 acres, respectively, in the area of present-day Breckin-ridge), Allen H. Thompson (160 acres in what is now Lincoln township), and Randolph McDonald (200 acres in what is now Grant township).

In all, twenty individuals bought land both prior to the end of 1838 and after the beginning of 1840 (see map 14). Many of these, like McGee, were old non-Mormon settlers. Others, however, were probably Mormons or Mormon dissenters who did not leave during the general exodus. This last group included John Corrill (who bought land in the county thru 1856), George Walter (buying land thru 1851), John H. Ardinger (buying land thru 1857), and Granville Jones (buying land thru 1852). One prominent Mormon dissenter who we known lived out his life in Caldwell County, John Whitmer, does not appear in the Land Records after 1837. When the majority of the Saints left, Whitmer returned to the ghost town of Far West and he continued to acquire land. This land, however, was not purchased from the Federal government but from Mormons who had left or from other third parties.

Mapping Settlements and Roads

T HE POPULATION OF northwestern Missouri in the 1830s was relatively small, but increasing rapidly. The most settled county in the region was Clay, whose population increased from 5,338 in 1830 to 8,533 in 1836 — a 63% increase in just six years.[28] Meanwhile Clinton County, which had been a part of Clay in 1830, was detached by 1836 and already boasted its own population of 1,890 residents. The 1836 populations

---

membered that "McGee & 2 sons" were part of the "Mob" who had "entered into an Agreement to drive the Mormons," Johnson, *Mormon Redress Petitions*, 526.

[28] Alphonso Wetmore, *Gazetteer of the State of Missouri* (St. Louis: C. Keemle, 1837), 267.

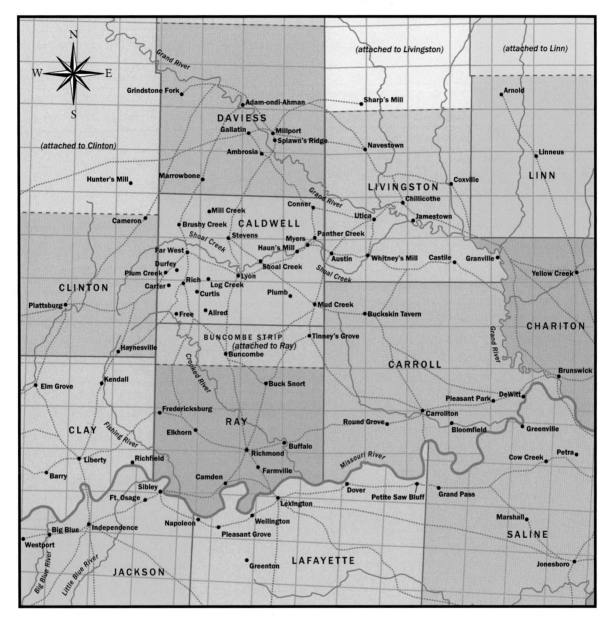

MAP 15: Settlements and roads in northwestern Missouri, 1838.

for the other counties in the region were Ray: 6,573, Lafayette: 4,683, Jackson: 4,522, Chariton: 3,483, Saline: 3,421, and Carroll: 2,122.[29] Between 1836 and 1839 these populations continued to increase. Although Clay lost several thousand residents as its

---

[29] Ibid. Because Caldwell and Daviess Counties were only organized in 1836 and Livingston and Linn Counties in 1837, the Gazetteer does not estimate their 1836 populations separately from the counties they had been attached to: Ray, Ray,k Carroll, and Randolph Counties, respectively.

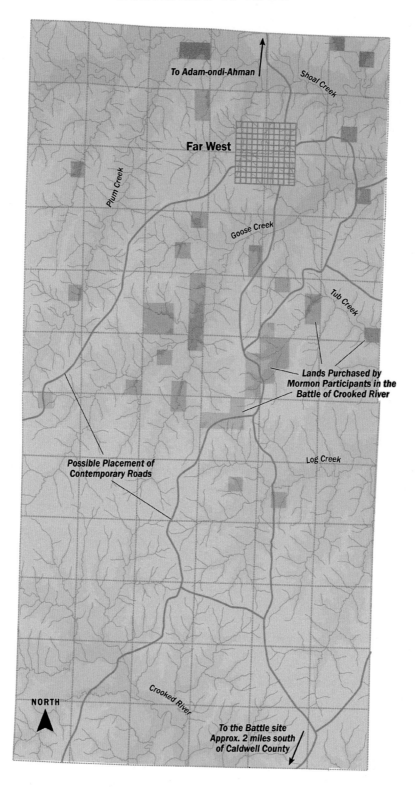

MAP 16: The lands owned by known Mormon participants in the Battle of Crooked River. Contemporary roads probably followed ridges between the creekbeds of Caldwell County, making as few fords as possible.

Mormon population relocated to Caldwell and elsewhere, this loss was quickly replaced by new non-Mormon immigrants.[30] Although only organized in 1837, Livingston County filled quickly, achieving a population of 4,325 by 1840. Daviess, likewise, experienced a rapid influx, attracting perhaps 1,000 non-Mormon residents by the summer of 1838 as many as 2,000 Mormon residents. The most rapid growth of all, however, occurred in Caldwell County, where the population increased to between 5,000 and 7,000 by the summer of 1838.

The combination of the land record data and the terrain data has also begun to help historians piece together the answers to other geographical questions: for example, where were the principal roads or paths that used during the Mormon period? (See map 15.) What was the path used for settlers coming from the East, traveling up the Missouri to the Grand River and thence to Haun's Mill and Far West? Where was the route from Ray County through Far West and up to Adam-ondi-Ahman? From the written sources we know that these primarily followed the ridges between creeks, making as few fords as possible. The maps help us see that terrain in relation to property owned in the Mormon period. Using these, in connection with the written sources and the few contemporary maps that show roads, we are able to estimate the most likely routes. In the lead-up to the battle between Mormon and Missourian militias at Crooked River, just outside of Caldwell County, for example, Mormon forces traveled south from Far West quickly along the main roads or paths. On the way, Mormon leader Charles C. Rich collected a number of participants. When the farms purchased by known Mormon participants in the battle are highlighted many are found to be along the likeliest path between Far West and Crooked River (see map 16).[31]

Also evident on the maps are outlying clusters of purchased property (see map 17). Some of these highlight known settlements like the Haun's Mill, Mill Creek, and Guyman's Horse Mill settlements. Other concentrations pinpoint lesser known locations for historians to identify in conjunction with the written sources. (Indeed, since the publication of the previous edition of *Northeast of Eden,* two new surveys have mapped Caldwell County settlement and proposed to identify outlying settlements.)[32]

---

[30] According to the 1840 census, Clay County had a total population of 8,282, just a few hundred fewer than its 1836 total.

[31] For a list of the participants, see Baugh, *A Call to Arms,* 197–202.

[32] Two important, independent surveys of Caldwell County have subsequently appeared. The first is LaMar C. Berrett and Max H. Parkin's long-awaited guide *Sacred Places, Vol. 4: Missouri: A Comprehensive*

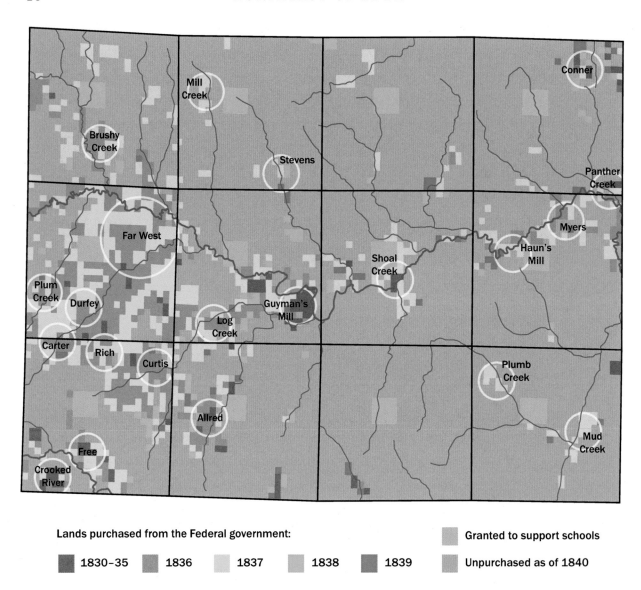

MAP 17: Land purchase clusters may make it possible to speculate about outlying settlements in Caldwell County.

One additional comparison the Caldwell County Land Record maps make possible is speculation that certain Saints were each other's neighbors. Such neighborhood ties might be useful to help explain later connections between families that migrated together and/or intermarried with one another. For example, this map shows that Lettice Palmer,

---

Guide to Early LDS Historical Sites, 286–357. The second is Jeffrey N. Walker's "Mormon Land Rights in Caldwell and Daviess Counties and the Mormon Conflict of 1838: New Findings and New Understandings," *BYU Studies* 47:1 (2008), 4–55.

John Whitmer 11-2-36	Lettice Palmer 12-7-36	Joel Schearer 11-25-36	Henry Wood 9-20-32	John Whitmer 8-8-36	Daniel Shearer 9-24-36	Daniel C. Davis 9-30-36	Joseph W. Younger 9-13-36	Joseph W. Younger 5-8-37	John Daley 5-22-37	John Daley 5-22-37	John Daley 5-22-37
John Whitmer 11-2-36	Lettice Palmer 12-7-36	Joel Schearer 11-25-36	Joel Schearer 8-11-36	John Whitmer 8-8-36	Daniel Shearer 9-24-36	Jerome M. Benson 8-18-36	Timothy B. Clark 10-11-36	Joseph W. Younger 5-8-37	John Daley 5-22-37	John Daley 5-22-37	John Daley 5-22-37
Edward Partridge 7-25-37	Warren Graves 11-26-36	Joseph Smith, Jr. 6-22-36	George Bebe 8-8-36	Jesse Cleavinger Jr. 8-27-35	George Beebe 8-8-36	Alban Allen 9-24-36	Jerome M. Benson 10-20-36	Samuel Miles 2-21-37	John Daley 5-22-37	John Daley 5-22-37	John Daley 5-22-37
Alvin C. Graves 11-3-36	Alvin C. Graves 8-12-36	Joseph Smith, Jr. 6-22-36	George Bebe 8-8-36	Jesse Cleavinger Jr. 8-27-35	Calvin Beebe 8-15-36	Solomon Daniels 11-29-36	Solomon Daniels 1-19-37	Samuel Miles 2-21-37	John Daley 5-22-37	John Daley 5-22-37	John Daley 5-22-37
Joseph Smith, Jr. 6-22-36	Joseph Smith, Jr. 6-22-36	Joseph Smith, Jr. 6-22-36	Isaac Beebe 9-6-36	Ambrose Palmer 9-8-36	Gad Yale 10-24-36	Porter Rockwell 2-13-37	Orrin Phelps 2-15-37	Julius Beech 8-22-36	Samuel Miles 6-19-37	William Frye 9-8-36	Elisha Alvord 11-21-37
Joseph Smith, Jr. 6-22-36	Joseph Smith, Jr. 6-22-36	Joseph Smith, Jr. 6-22-36	Reed Peck 9-24-36	Ambrose Palmer 9-8-36	Calvin Beebe 5-3-37	Orrin Phelps 6-10-37	Morris Phelps 8-25-36	Julius Beech 8-22-36	Thomas Huntsacker 9-19-35	William Frye 9-8-36	George Johnson 9-11-37
Joseph Smith, Jr. 6-22-36	Joseph Smith, Jr. 6-22-36	John Higbee 5-2-37	John Higbee 8-11-36	Chester C. Thornton 5-9-37	John L. Butler 6-12-37	John L. Butler 6-17-37	Morris Phelps 8-25-36	Oliver Cowdery 6-22-36	Oliver Cowdery 6-22-36	Daniel Guyun 1-10-35	John Daley 5-22-37
Joseph Smith, Jr. 6-22-36	Joseph Smith, Jr. 6-22-36	Moses Martin 9-20-36	John Higbee 8-11-36	James Emet 6-17-37	John L. Butler 6-12-37	Samuel Kimbel 3-3-36		Oliver Cowdery 6-22-36	Oliver Cowdery 6-22-36	Daniel Guyun 1-10-35	Jefferson Hunt 2-6-37

MAP 18: The land purchases maps in this atlas highlight potential neighbors.

Joel Scherer, Warren Graves, Alvin C. Graves, George Beebe, Isaac Beebe, Calvin Beebe, Ambrose Palmer, Reed Peck, Gad Yale, and Porter Rockwell (among others) all bought land in the same area (see map 18). Do they share any other connections? The maps open up numerous possibilities for new comparisons. This information, however, must be treated with special caution because the land records alone are not proof that the owner ever lived on the property: much of the land was bought for speculation and many owners bought multiple farms. Additionally, because no subsequent sales of the land are recorded, we cannot know from the maps alone who may have lived on any given parcel at any given time. But coupled with references in other written sources, this information can give us intriguing hints at potential connections between individual Saints.

In the end, new maps allow historians to organize and synthesize information in new ways, highlighting connections that may be obscure in the literary record alone. It is hoped that this atlas will contribute to our understanding of this brief, but transformative period in the history of Mormonism.

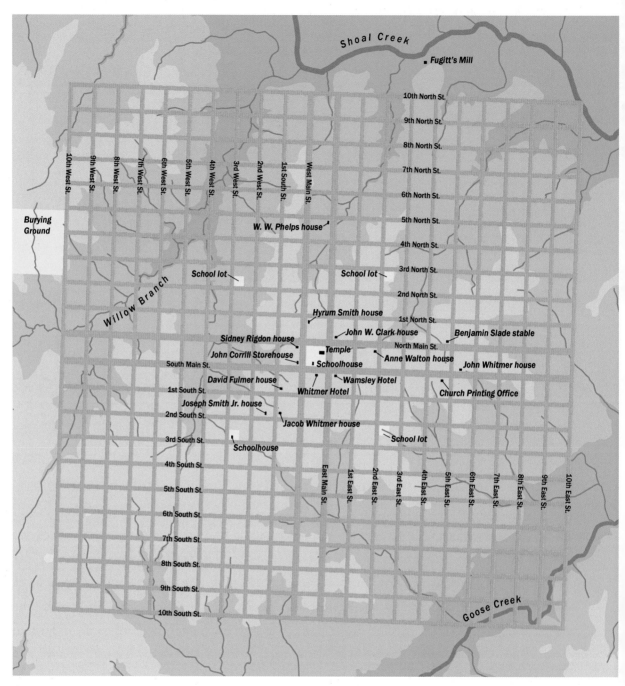

Shoal Creek

■ Fugitt's Mill

10th North St.

9th North St.

8th North St.

7th North St.

6th North St.

5th North St.

4th North St.

W. W. Phelps house

School lot   School lot   3rd North St.

2nd North St.

Hyrum Smith house   1st North St.

John W. Clark house   Benjamin Slade stable

Sidney Rigdon house   Temple   North Main St.

John Corrill Storehouse   Schoolhouse   Anne Walton house   John Whitmer house

South Main St.   Wamsley Hotel

David Fulmer house   Whitmer Hotel

1st South St.   Church Printing Office

Joseph Smith Jr. house

2nd South St.   Jacob Whitmer house

3rd South St.   School lot

Schoolhouse

4th South St.

5th South St.

6th South St.

7th South St.

8th South St.

9th South St.

10th South St.

Burying Ground

Willow Branch

Goose Creek

10th West St. · 9th West St. · 8th West St. · 7th West St. · 6th West St. · 5th West St. · 4th West St. · 3rd West St. · 2nd West St. · 1st South St. · West Main St.

East Main St. · 1st East St. · 2nd East St. · 3rd East St. · 4th East St. · 5th East St. · 6th East St. · 7th East St. · 8th East St. · 9th East St. · 10th East St.

Sites in Far West

N
W · E
S

Miles

0   0.5   1.0

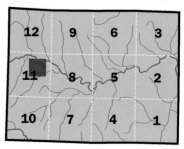

12	9	6	3
11	8	5	2
10	7	4	1

Area enlarged above

Using this Atlas

THE MAPS ON PAGES 30–31 are a reference which shows how Caldwell County has been divided into forty-eight maps on pages 32 to 79 of this atlas. For the purposes of the atlas, each of the county's twelve statute townships has been divided into quarters (NW, NE, SW and SE).[33] Each quarter township has its own page beginning on page 32 in the extreme northwestern corner of the county and then moving left to right (west to east) until the entire row is finished. Since the atlas finishes the entire row of quarter townships before moving south to the next row, the northern half of each township is separated from the southern half, e.g. the northern part of Township 12 is on pages 32–33 while the southern part is on pages 40–41. Also, because the townships themselves are numbered north and west (i.e., from the bottom and then to the left) from the 5th Principal Meridian and Baseline (see map 7 on page 12), while the atlas moves from west to east and north to south (i.e., left to right and top to bottom), the atlas actually maps Township 12 first and Township 1 last. This is a concession to modern spatial conceptions and conventions which are rather different from those used in the early 19th century.

The maps show current terrain data including creeks derived from the United States Geological Service (USGS). Obviously some changes will have occurred since the late 1830s. The maps also show contemporary roads and towns. Overlaid on this base are the section numbers and lines and divisions down to each quarter quarter section. Many lines in the maps are skewed because the original 19th survey grid diverges from the true cardinal directions. Finally, in each quarter quarter section purchased by 1839, the name of the purchaser and date of purchase is listed. Empty quarter quarter sections remained unpurchased as of the beginning of 1840.

---

[33] Please note that a "quarter township" is not a legal division or unit. I have only made these divisions because of the size constraints of the page and for legibility of the type.

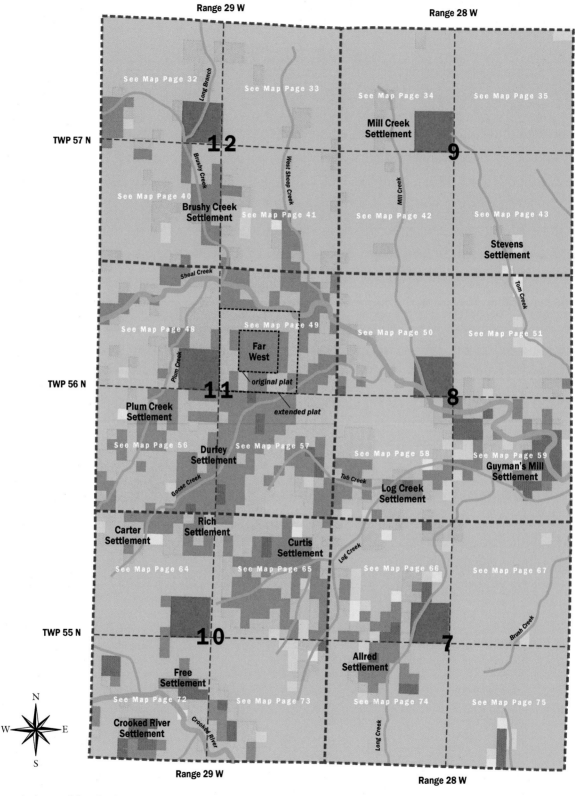

Range 29 W   Range 28 W

See Map Page 32   See Map Page 33   See Map Page 34   See Map Page 35

Long Branch

Mill Creek
Settlement

TWP 57 N   **12**   **9**

Brushy Creek

West Sheep Creek

Mill Creek

See Map Page 40   Brushy Creek Settlement   See Map Page 41   See Map Page 42   See Map Page 43

Stevens
Settlement

Shoal Creek

Tom Creek

See Map Page 48   See Map Page 49   See Map Page 50   See Map Page 51

Far
West

Plum Creek

original plat

TWP 56 N   **11**   extended plat   **8**

Plum Creek
Settlement

See Map Page 56   Durley Settlement   See Map Page 57   See Map Page 58   See Map Page 59

Goose Creek   Tub Creek   Guyman's Mill
Settlement

Log Creek
Settlement

Carter
Settlement   Rich
Settlement   Curtis
Settlement

Log Creek

See Map Page 64   See Map Page 65   See Map Page 66   See Map Page 67

TWP 55 N   **10**   **7**

Free
Settlement

Allred
Settlement

Brush Creek

See Map Page 72   See Map Page 73   See Map Page 74   See Map Page 75

Crooked River
Settlement

Crooked River

Long Creek

N
W   E
S

Range 29 W   Range 28 W

Caldwell County
[Western Half]

Lands Purchased from the Federal Government

■ School lands   ■ 1830-35   ■ 1836   ■ 1837   ■ 1838   ■ 1839   ■ After 1839

Range 27 W

Range 26 W

Lick Fork

See Map Page 36

See Map Page 37

See Map Page 38

See Map Page 39

Conner
Settlement

6

3

TWP 57 N

Little Otter Creek

See Map Page 44

See Map Page 45

See Map Page 46

See Map Page 47

Panther Creek

Cottonwood Creek

Otter Creek

See Map Page 52

See Map Page 53

See Map Page 54

See Map Page 55

Myers
Settlement

Shoal Creek

Haun's Mill
Settlement

5

2

TWP 56 N

Shoal Creek

Shoal Creek
Settlement

See Map Page 60

See Map Page 61

See Map Page 62

See Map Page 63

Dead Oak Branch

Crabapple Creek

See Map Page 68

See Map Page 69

See Map Page 70

See Map Page 71

North Mud Creek

Mud Creek

4

1

TWP 55 N

Mud Creek
Settlement

See Map Page 76

See Map Page 77

See Map Page 78

See Map Page 79

Range 27 W

Range 26 W

Miles

0   2   4

Caldwell County
[Eastern Half]

DAVIESS COUNTY

County St.

3   **4**   **5**

6

5

4

Owen D. Stout
2-21-37

Owen D. Stout
2-9-37

Philo Dibble
9-21-37

James Annis
2-17-37

Owen D. Stout
2-9-37

Philo Dibble
9-21-37

Jordan Branch

NW Santa Rosa

NW Sale/Barn Rd.

NW Joe Montana Rd.

NW Center Rd.

John C. Annis
2-14-37

15   7   **16**   8   **17**

John C. Annis
2-14-37

James Annis
2-17-37

9

474

Samuel Egbert
1-17-37

1

2

Long Branch

Samuel Shepherd
2-14-37

DEKALB COUNTY (founded in 1843)

NE TOWNSHIP 12 (see page 33)

George W. Parker
11-17-36

John Patten
11-11-36

George Carson
9-6-36

Brushy Creek

Joshua Fairchild
7-13-37

(School)

(School)

NW Thiel Dr.

(School)

(School)

George W. Parker
11-17-36

John Patten
11-11-36

William H. Carson
3-18-37

Joshua Fairchild
7-13-37

(School)

(School)

(School)

(School)

William G. McDaniel
5-12-36

1=8

George W. Parker
11-17-36

Benjamin Middaugh
4-9-39

1=7

36

(School)

(School)

1=6

(School)

(School)

William G. McDaniel
5-12-36

George W. Parker
11-17-36

John Archer
8-8-37

NW Old US 36 Rd.

(School)

(School)

(School)

(School)

475

(School)

(School)

(School)

(School)

475

SW TOWNSHIP 12 (see page 40)

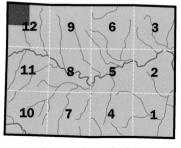

12   9   6   3

11   8   5   2

10   7   4   1

Area enlarged above

TOWNSHIP 12

[Kidder, NW]

Miles

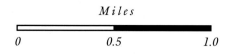

0   0.5   1.0

N
W   E
S

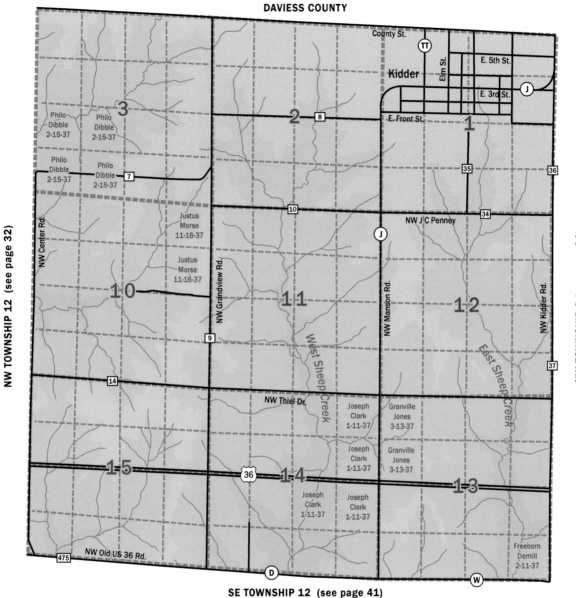

TOWNSHIP 12

[Kidder, NE]

Miles

0   0.5   1.0

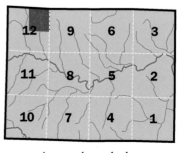

Area enlarged above

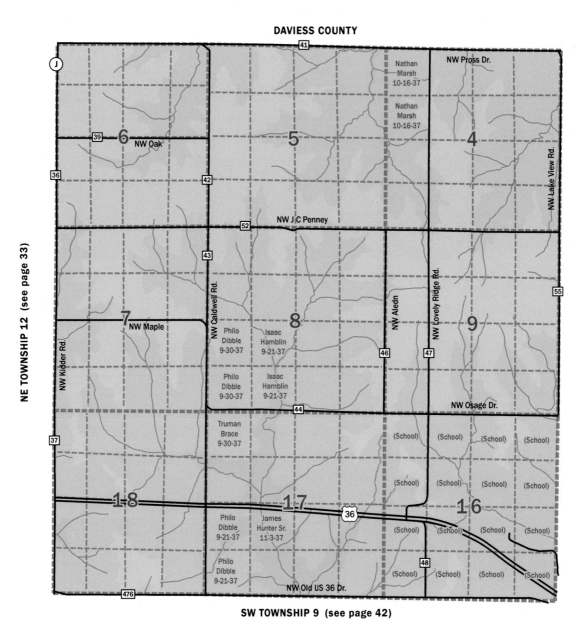

DAVIESS COUNTY

NE TOWNSHIP 12 (see page 33)

NE TOWNSHIP 9 (see page 35)

SW TOWNSHIP 9 (see page 42)

41

J

39 6 NW Oak

5

NW Pross Dr.

Nathan Marsh 10-16-37

Nathan Marsh 10-16-37

4

36

42

NW-Lake View Rd.

52 NW J C Penney

43

7 NW Maple

NW Caldwell Rd.

NW Kidder Rd.

8

Philo Dibble 9-30-37

Isaac Hamblin 9-21-37

Philo Dibble 9-30-37

Isaac Hamblin 9-21-37

NW Aledn

46

NW Lovely Ridge Rd.

47

9

55

NW Osage Dr.

44

37

Truman Brace 9-30-37

(School) (School) (School) (School)

(School) (School) (School) (School)

1-8

17

36

1-6

Philo Dibble 9-21-37

James Hunter Sr. 11-3-37

(School) (School) (School) (School)

Philo Dibble 9-21-37

48

(School) (School) (School) (School)

NW Old US 36 Dr.

476

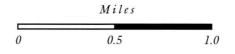

TOWNSHIP 9

[Kingston, NW]

12　9　6　3

11　8　5　2

10　7　4　1

Area enlarged above

Miles

0　　　　0.5　　　　1.0

N W E S

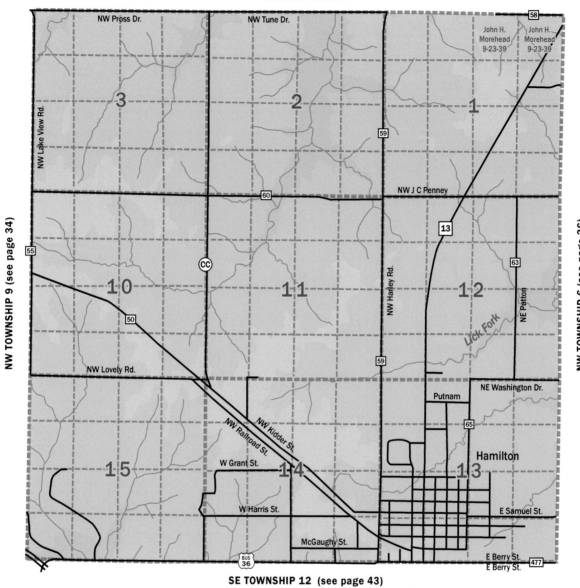

DAVIESS COUNTY

NW Pross Dr.

NW Tune Dr.

John H. Morehead 9-23-39

John H. Morehead 9-23-39

3

2

1

NW Lake View Rd.

NW J C Penney

NW TOWNSHIP 9 (see page 34)

NW TOWNSHIP 6 (see page 36)

CC

10

11

12

NW Harley Rd.

NE Patton

Lick Fork

NW Lovely Rd.

NE Washington Dr.

NW Railroad St.

NW Kidder St.

Putnam

Hamilton

15

W Grant St.

14

13

W Harris St.

E Samuel St.

McGaughy St.

E Berry St.
E Berry St.

SE TOWNSHIP 12 (see page 43)

TOWNSHIP 9

[Hamilton, NE]

N
W   E
S

Miles

0   0.5   1.0

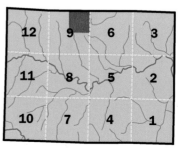

12	9	6	3
11	8	5	2
10	7	4	1

Area enlarged above

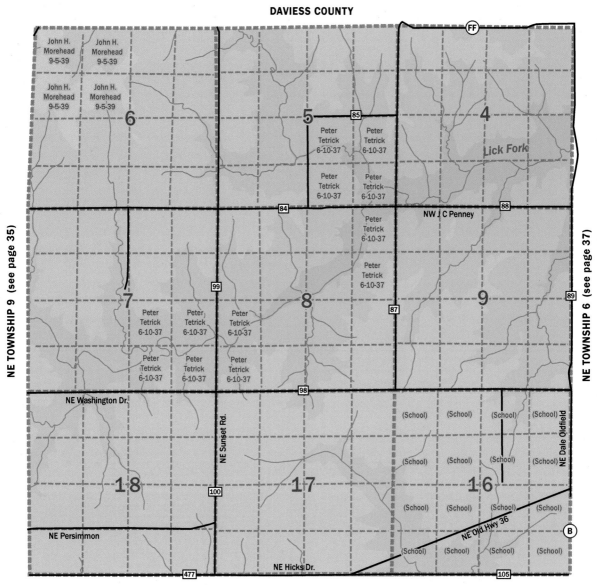

DAVIESS COUNTY

John H. Morehead 9-5-39 | John H. Morehead 9-5-39

John H. Morehead 9-5-39 | John H. Morehead 9-5-39

6

5 [85] 4

Lick Fork

Peter Tetrick 6-10-37 | Peter Tetrick 6-10-37

Peter Tetrick 6-10-37 | Peter Tetrick 6-10-37

[84]

NW J C Penney [88]

Peter Tetrick 6-10-37

Peter Tetrick 6-10-37

NE TOWNSHIP 9 (see page 35)

NE TOWNSHIP 6 (see page 37)

[99]

7 8 9 [89]

Peter Tetrick 6-10-37 | Peter Tetrick 6-10-37 | Peter Tetrick 6-10-37 [87]

Peter Tetrick 6-10-37 | Peter Tetrick 6-10-37 | Peter Tetrick 6-10-37

[98]

NE Washington Dr.

(School) | (School) | (School) | (School)

(School) | (School) | (School) | (School)

NE Sunset Rd.

NE Dale Oldfield

18 [100] 17 16

(School) | (School) | (School) | (School)

NE Persimmon

NE Old Hwy 36 [B]

NE Hicks Dr.

(School) | (School) | (School) | (School)

[477] [105]

SW TOWNSHIP 6 (see page 44)

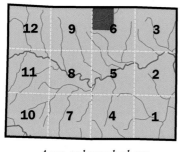

12	9	6	3
11	8	5	2
10	7	4	1

Area enlarged above

TOWNSHIP 6

[Gomer, NW]

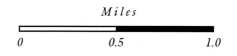

Miles

0   0.5   1.0

N
W   E
S

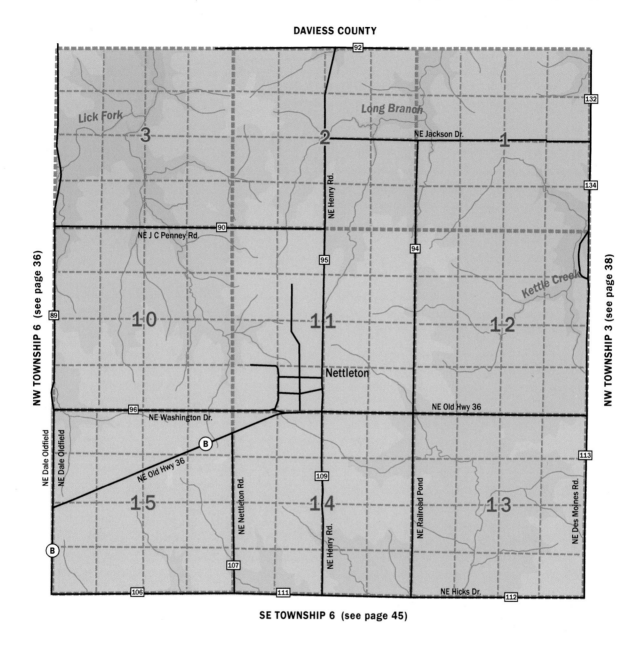

DAVIESS COUNTY

Lick Fork

Long Branch

NE Jackson Dr.

3

2

1

NE Henry Rd.

NE J C Penney Rd.

Kettle Creek

10

11

12

Nettleton

NE Old Hwy 36

NE Washington Dr.

NE Old Hwy 36

NE Dale Oldfield

NE Dale Oldfield

NE Nettleton Rd.

NE Henry Rd.

NE Railroad Pond

NE Des Moines Rd.

15

14

13

NE Hicks Dr.

NW TOWNSHIP 6 (see page 36)

NW TOWNSHIP 3 (see page 38)

SE TOWNSHIP 6 (see page 45)

TOWNSHIP 6

[Gomer, NE]

Miles

0   0.5   1.0

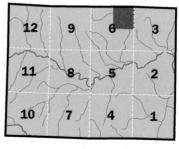

Area enlarged above

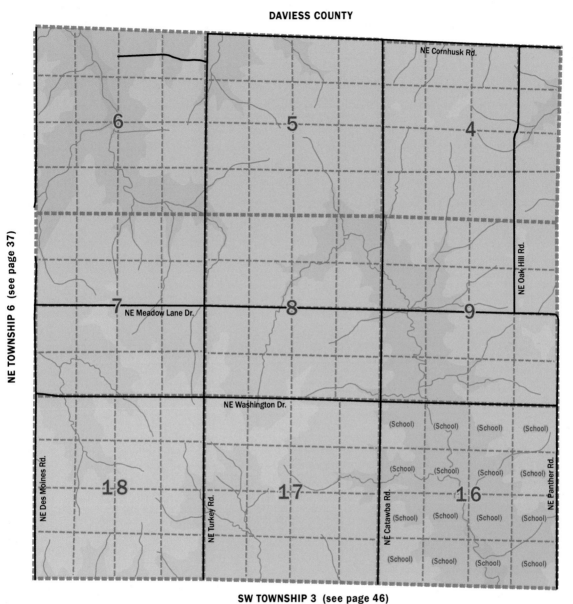

DAVIESS COUNTY

6

5

4

NE Cornhusk Rd.

NE TOWNSHIP 6 (see page 37)

NE TOWNSHIP 3 (see page 39)

NE Oak Hill Rd.

7

NE Meadow Lane Dr.

8

9

NE Washington Dr.

18

17

16

NE Des Moines Rd.

NE Turkey Rd.

NE Catawba Rd.

NE Panther Rd.

(School) (School) (School) (School)

(School) (School) (School) (School)

(School) (School) (School) (School)

(School) (School) (School) (School)

SW TOWNSHIP 3 (see page 46)

12	9	6	3
11	8	5	2
10	7	4	1

Area enlarged above

TOWNSHIP 3

[Breckenridge, NW]

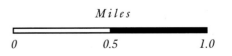

Miles

0   0.5   1.0

N
W   E
S

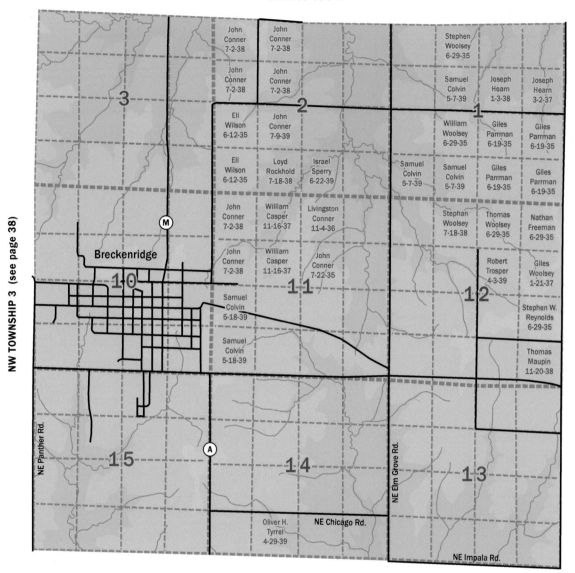

DAVIESS COUNTY

NW TOWNSHIP 3 (see page 38)

LIVINGSTON COUNTY

John Conner 7-2-38	John Conner 7-2-38	
John Conner 7-2-38	John Conner 7-2-38	Stephen Woolsey 6-29-35
		Samuel Colvin 5-7-39 / Joseph Hearn 1-3-38 / Joseph Hearn 3-2-37

3

2

1

Eli Wilson 6-12-35 / John Conner 7-9-39

William Woolsey 6-29-35 / Giles Parrman 6-19-35 / Giles Parrman 6-19-35

Eli Wilson 6-12-35 / Loyd Rockhold 7-18-38 / Israel Sperry 6-22-39

Samuel Colvin 5-7-39 / Samuel Colvin 5-7-39 / Giles Parrman 6-19-35 / Giles Parrman 6-19-35

John Conner 7-2-38 / William Casper 11-16-37 / Livingston Conner 11-4-36

Stephan Woolsey 7-18-38 / Thomas Woolsey 6-29-35 / Nathan Freeman 6-29-35

Breckenridge

John Conner 7-2-38 / William Casper 11-16-37 / John Conner 7-22-35

Robert Trosper 4-3-39 / Giles Woolsey 1-21-37

10

11

12

Samuel Colvin 5-18-39

Stephen W. Reynolds 6-29-35

Samuel Colvin 5-18-39

Thomas Maupin 11-20-38

NE Panther Rd.

15

NE Elm Grove Rd.

14

13

Oliver H. Tyrrel 4-29-39   **NE Chicago Rd.**

NE Impala Rd.

SE TOWNSHIP 3 (see page 47)

TOWNSHIP 3

[Breckenridge, NE]

N
W — E
S

Miles

0	0.5	1.0

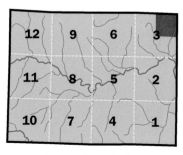

12	9	6	3
11	8	5	2
10	7	4	1

Area enlarged above

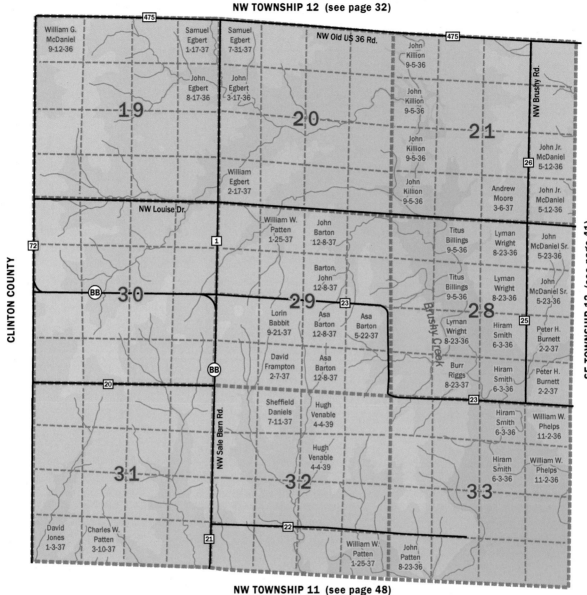

NW TOWNSHIP 12 (see page 32)

475

William G.
McDaniel
9-12-36

Samuel
Egbert
1-17-37

Samuel
Egbert
7-31-37

NW Old US 36 Rd.

John
Killion
9-5-36

475

John
Egbert
8-17-36

John
Egbert
3-17-36

19

John
Killion
9-5-36

NW Brushy Rd.

20

21

John
Killion
9-5-36

William
Egbert
2-17-37

26

John Jr.
McDaniel
5-12-36

John
Killion
9-5-36

Andrew
Moore
3-6-37

John Jr.
McDaniel
5-12-36

NW Louise Dr.

William W.
Patten
1-25-37

John
Barton
12-8-37

Titus
Billings
9-5-36

Lyman
Wright
8-23-36

John
McDaniel Sr.
5-23-36

72

1

Barton,
John
12-8-37

Titus
Billings
9-5-36

Lyman
Wright
8-23-36

John
McDaniel Sr.
5-23-36

BB

30

Lorin
Babbit
9-21-37

Asa
Barton
12-8-37

23

Asa
Barton
5-22-37

29

Lyman
Wright
8-23-36

28

Hiram
Smith
6-3-36

25

Peter H.
Burnett
2-2-37

BB

David
Frampton
2-7-37

Asa
Barton
12-8-37

Burr
Riggs
8-23-37

Hiram
Smith
6-3-36

Peter H.
Burnett
2-2-37

20

Sheffield
Daniels
7-11-37

Hugh
Venable
4-4-39

23

Hiram
Smith
6-3-36

William W.
Phelps
11-2-36

NW Sale Barn Rd.

Hugh
Venable
4-4-39

Hiram
Smith
6-3-36

William W.
Phelps
11-2-36

31

32

33

David
Jones
1-3-37

Charles W.
Patten
3-10-37

21

22

William W.
Patten
1-25-37

John
Patten
8-23-36

CLINTON COUNTY

SE TOWNSHIP 12 (see page 41)

Brushy Creek

NW TOWNSHIP 11 (see page 48)

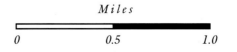

12	9	6	3
11	8	5	2
10	7	4	1

Area enlarged above

TOWNSHIP 12

[Kidder, SW]

Miles

0　　　　0.5　　　　1.0

N
W　E
S

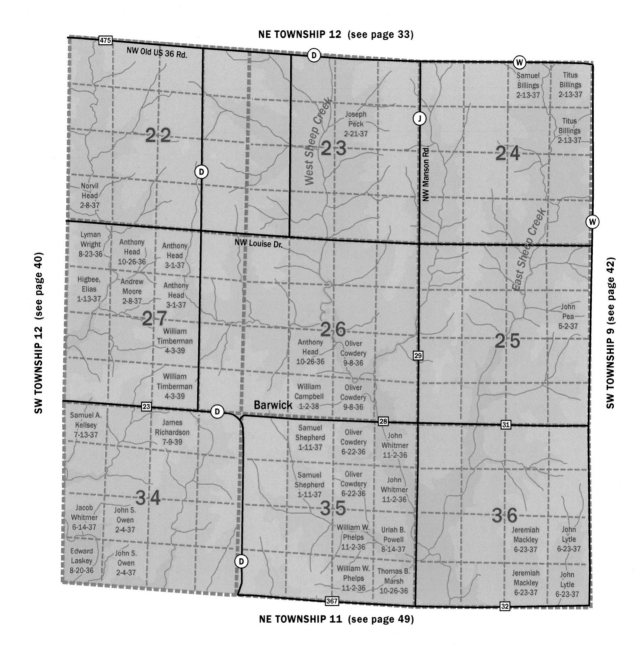

NE TOWNSHIP 12 (see page 33)

NW Old US 36 Rd.

475

D

W

Samuel
Billings
2-13-37

Titus
Billings
2-13-37

Joseph
Peck
2-21-37

Titus
Billings
2-13-37

J

2-2

West Sheep Creek

2-3

2-4

NW Manson Rd.

Norvil
Head
2-8-37

D

W

East Sheep Creek

NW Louise Dr.

SW TOWNSHIP 12 (see page 40)

SW TOWNSHIP 9 (see page 42)

Lyman
Wright
8-23-36

Anthony
Head
10-26-36

Anthony
Head
3-1-37

Higbee,
Elias
1-13-37

Andrew
Moore
2-8-37

Anthony
Head
3-1-37

John
Pea
5-2-37

2-7

William
Timberman
4-3-39

2-6

Anthony
Head
10-26-36

Oliver
Cowdery
9-8-36

2-5

29

William
Timberman
4-3-39

William
Campbell
1-2-38

Oliver
Cowdery
9-8-36

Barwick

D

28

31

Samuel A.
Kellsey
7-13-37

James
Richardson
7-9-39

Samuel
Shepherd
1-11-37

Oliver
Cowdery
6-22-36

John
Whitmer
11-2-36

Samuel
Shepherd
1-11-37

Oliver
Cowdery
6-22-36

John
Whitmer
11-2-36

23

D

3-4

Jacob
Whitmer
6-14-37

John S.
Owen
2-4-37

3-5

3-6

Jeremiah
Mackley
6-23-37

John
Lytle
6-23-37

Edward
Laskey
8-20-36

John S.
Owen
2-4-37

D

William W.
Phelps
11-2-36

Uriah B.
Powell
8-14-37

William W.
Phelps
11-2-36

Thomas B.
Marsh
10-26-36

Jeremiah
Mackley
6-23-37

John
Lytle
6-23-37

367

32

NE TOWNSHIP 11 (see page 49)

TOWNSHIP 12

[Kidder, SE]

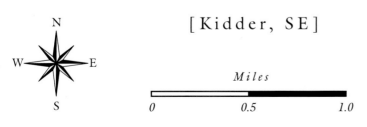

N
W   E
S

Miles

0   0.5   1.0

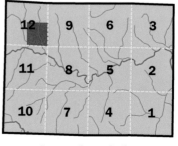

12	9	6	3
11	8	5	2
10	7	4	1

Area enlarged above

NW TOWNSHIP 9 (see page 34)

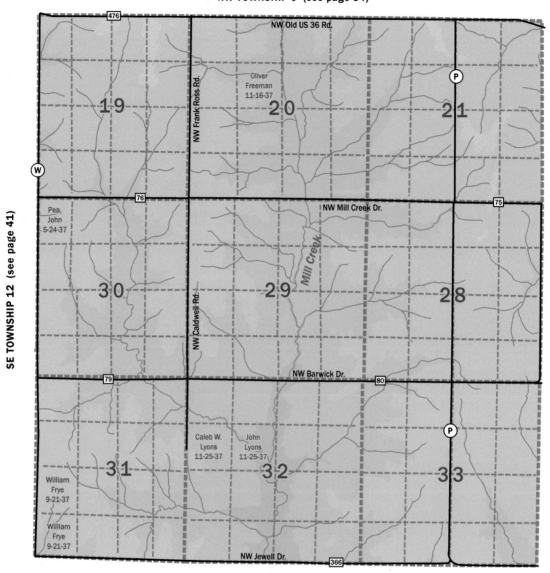

NW Old US 36 Rd.

476

NW Frank Ross Rd.

Oliver
Freeman
11-16-37

P

19   20   21

W

76

SE TOWNSHIP 12 (see page 41)

75

SE TOWNSHIP 9 (see page 43)

NW Mill Creek Dr.

Pea,
John
5-24-37

Mill Creek

NW Caldwell Rd.

30   29   28

79   NW Barwick Dr.   80

Caleb W.
Lyons
11-25-37

John
Lyons
11-25-37

P

31   32   33

William
Frye
9-21-37

William
Frye
9-21-37

NW Jewell Dr.   366

NW TOWNSHIP 8 (see page 50)

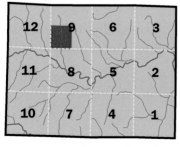

12	9	6	3
11	8	5	2
10	7	4	1

Area enlarged above

TOWNSHIP 9

[Hamilton, SW]

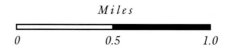

Miles

0   0.5   1.0

N
W   E
S

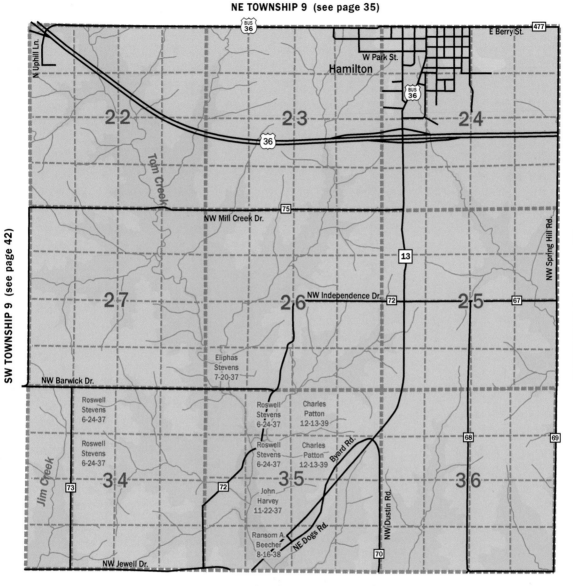

NE TOWNSHIP 9 (see page 35)

SW TOWNSHIP 9 (see page 42)

SW TOWNSHIP 6 (see page 44)

Hamilton

22   23   24

27   26   25

34   35   36

Eliphas Stevens 7-20-37

Roswell Stevens 6-24-37

Roswell Stevens 6-24-37

Roswell Stevens 6-24-37

Roswell Stevens 6-24-37

Charles Patton 12-13-39

Charles Patton 12-13-39

John Harvey 11-22-37

Ransom A. Beecher 8-16-38

NE TOWNSHIP 8 (see page 51)

TOWNSHIP 9

[Hamilton, SE]

Miles

0   0.5   1.0

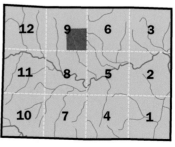

Area enlarged above

NW TOWNSHIP 6 (see page 36)

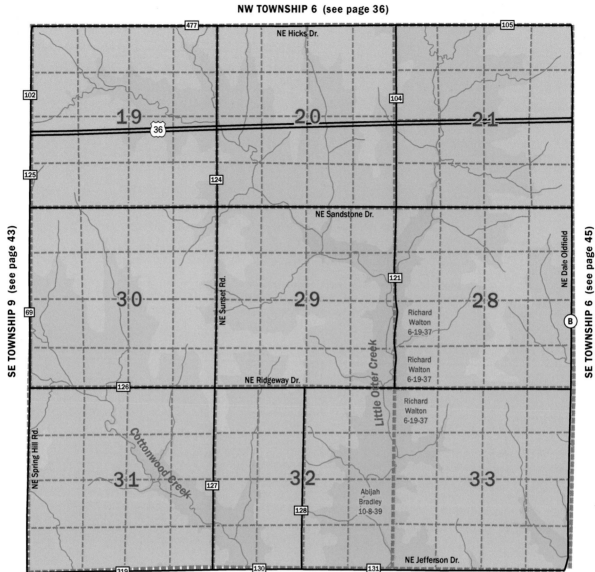

NE Hicks Dr.

477

105

102

19

104

20

21

36

125

124

SE TOWNSHIP 9 (see page 43)

NE Sandstone Dr.

69

30

NE Sunset Rd.

29

121

28

SE TOWNSHIP 6 (see page 45)

NE Dale Oldfield

Richard
Walton
6-19-37

Richard
Walton
6-19-37

NE Ridgeway Dr.

Little Otter Creek

B

126

Richard
Walton
6-19-37

NE Spring Hill Rd.

31

Cottonwood Creek

127

32

33

128

Abijah
Bradley
10-8-39

NE Jefferson Dr.

319

130

131

NW TOWNSHIP 5 (see page 52)

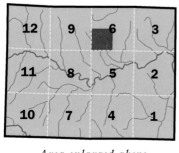

12	9	6	3
11	8	5	2
10	7	4	1

Area enlarged above

TOWNSHIP 6

[Gomer, SW]

N
W — E
S

Miles

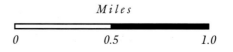

0   0.5   1.0

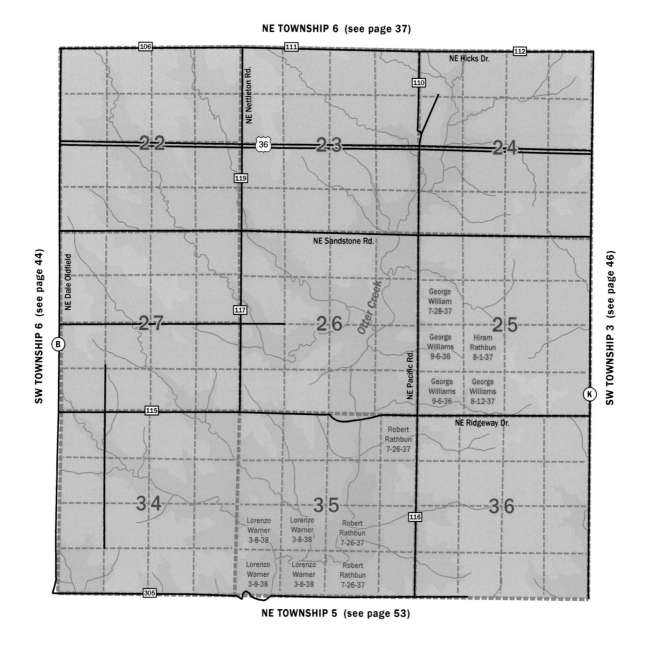

NE TOWNSHIP 6 (see page 37)

NE Hicks Dr.

NE Nettleton Rd.

22   23   24

NE Sandstone Rd.

SW TOWNSHIP 6 (see page 44)

NE Dale Oldfield

SW TOWNSHIP 3 (see page 46)

27   26   25

George
William
7-28-37

George
Williams
9-6-36

Hiram
Rathbun
8-1-37

NE Pacific Rd.

George
Williams
9-6-36

George
Williams
8-12-37

Robert
Rathbun
7-26-37

NE Ridgeway Dr.

34   35   36

Lorenzo
Warner
3-8-38

Lorenzo
Warner
3-8-38

Robert
Rathbun
7-26-37

Lorenzo
Warner
3-8-38

Lorenzo
Warner
3-8-38

Robert
Rathbun
7-26-37

NE TOWNSHIP 5 (see page 53)

TOWNSHIP 6

[Gomer, SE]

N
W   E
S

Miles

0   0.5   1.0

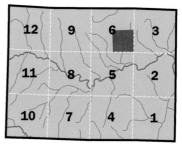

12	9	6	3
11	8	5	2
10	7	4	1

Area enlarged above

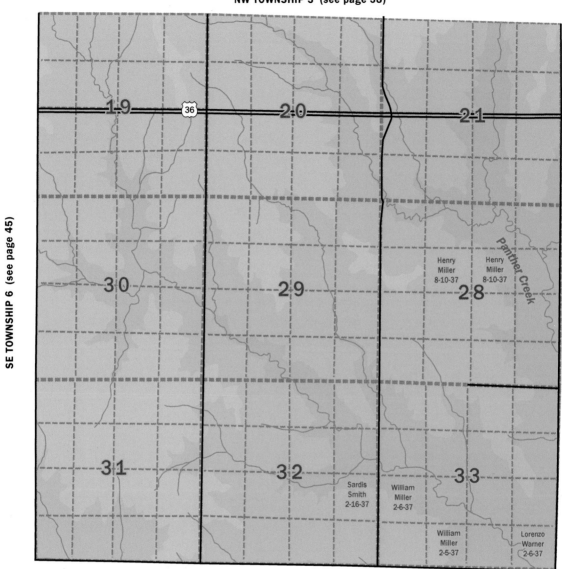

NW TOWNSHIP 3 (see page 38)

SE TOWNSHIP 6 (see page 45)

SE TOWNSHIP 3 (see page 47)

19

36

20

21

30

29

Henry
Miller
8-10-37

Henry
Miller
8-10-37

Panther Creek

28

31

32

Sardis
Smith
2-16-37

William
Miller
2-6-37

33

William
Miller
2-5-37

Lorenzo
Warner
2-6-37

NW TOWNSHIP 2 (see page 54)

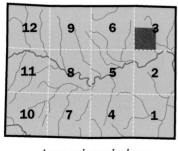

12	9	6	3
11	8	5	2
10	7	4	1

Area enlarged above

TOWNSHIP 3

[Breckenridge, SW]

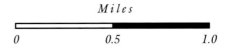

Miles

0   0.5   1.0

N
W   E
S

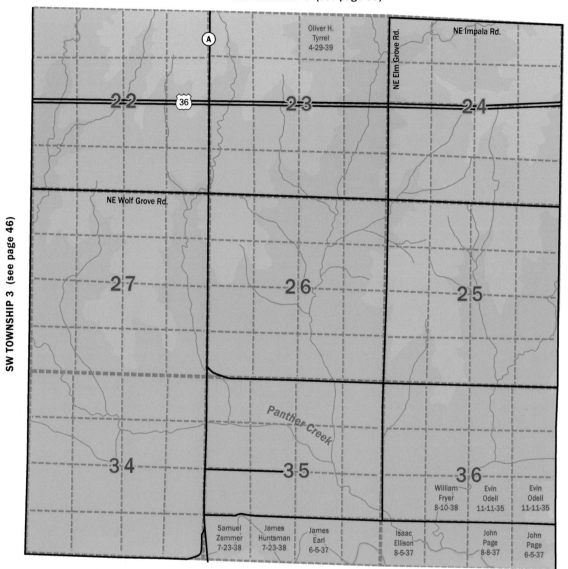

NE TOWNSHIP 3 (see page 39)

NE Impala Rd.

Oliver H. Tyrrel
4-29-39

NE Elm Grove Rd.

NE Wolf Grove Rd.

SW TOWNSHIP 3 (see page 46)

LIVINGSTON COUNTY

22   23   24

27   26   25

Panther Creek

34   35   36

William Fryer
8-10-38

Evin Odell
11-11-35

Evin Odell
11-11-35

Samuel Zemmer
7-23-38

James Huntsman
7-23-38

James Earl
6-5-37

Isaac Ellison
8-5-37

John Page
8-8-37

John Page
6-5-37

NE TOWNSHIP 2 (see page 55)

TOWNSHIP 3

[Breckenridge, SE]

N
W   E
S

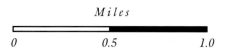

Miles

0   0.5   1.0

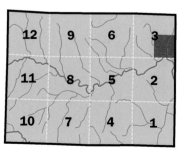

12	9	6	3
11	8	5	2
10	7	4	1

Area enlarged above

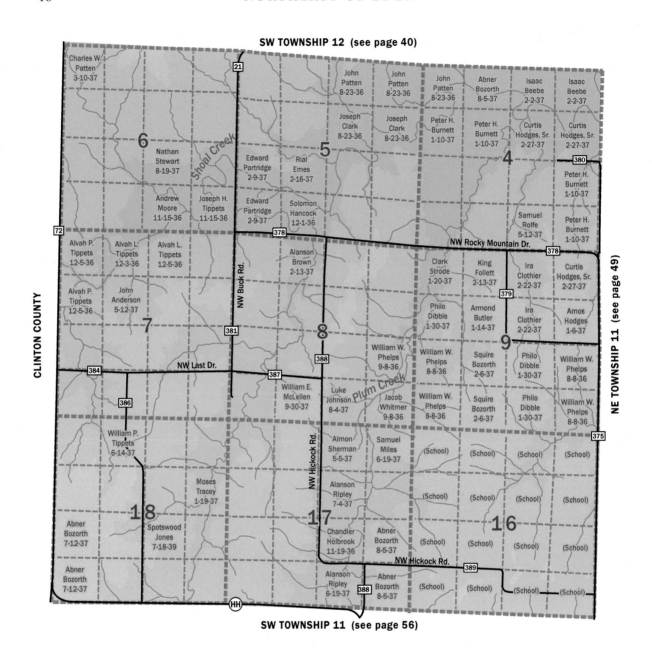

SW TOWNSHIP 12 (see page 40)

Charles W.
Patten
3-10-37

John
Patten
8-23-36

John
Patten
8-23-36

John
Patten
8-23-36

Abner
Bozorth
8-5-37

Isaac
Beebe
2-2-37

Isaac
Beebe
2-2-37

Joseph
Clark
8-23-36

Joseph
Clark
8-23-36

Peter H.
Burnett
1-10-37

Peter H.
Burnett
1-10-37

Curtis
Hodges, Sr.
2-27-37

Curtis
Hodges, Sr.
2-27-37

6

Nathan
Stewart
8-19-37

5

Edward
Partridge
2-9-37

Rial
Emes
2-16-37

4

Peter H.
Burnett
1-10-37

Andrew
Moore
11-15-36

Joseph H.
Tippets
11-15-36

Edward
Partridge
2-9-37

Solomon
Hancock
12-1-36

Samuel
Rolfe
5-12-37

Peter H.
Burnett
1-10-37

NW Rocky Mountain Dr.

Alvah P.
Tippets
12-5-36

Alvah L.
Tippets
12-3-36

Alvah L.
Tippets
12-5-36

Alanson
Brown
2-13-37

Clark
Strode
1-20-37

King
Follett
2-13-37

Ira
Clothier
2-22-37

Curtis
Hodges, Sr.
2-27-37

Alvah P.
Tippets
12-5-36

John
Anderson
5-12-37

7

Philo
Dibble
1-30-37

Armond
Butler
1-14-37

Ira
Clothier
2-22-37

Amos
Hodges
1-6-37

8

William W.
Phelps
9-8-36

William W.
Phelps
8-8-36

Squire
Bozorth
2-6-37

9

Philo
Dibble
1-30-37

William W.
Phelps
8-8-36

NW Last Dr.

William E.
McLellen
9-30-37

Luke
Johnson
8-4-37

Jacob
Whitmer
9-8-36

William W.
Phelps
8-8-36

Squire
Bozorth
2-6-37

Philo
Dibble
1-30-37

William W.
Phelps
8-8-36

William P.
Tippets
6-14-37

Almon
Sherman
5-5-37

Samuel
Miles
6-19-37

(School)

(School)

(School)

(School)

Moses
Tracey
1-19-37

Alanson
Ripley
7-4-37

(School)

(School)

(School)

(School)

18

Spotswood
Jones
7-18-39

17

Chandler
Holbrook
11-19-36

Abner
Bozorth
8-5-37

16

(School)

(School)

(School)

(School)

Abner
Bozorth
7-12-37

NW Hickock Rd.

Abner
Bozorth
7-12-37

Alanson
Ripley
6-19-37

Abner
Bozorth
8-5-37

(School)

(School)

(School)

(School)

SW TOWNSHIP 11 (see page 56)

CLINTON COUNTY

Shoal Creek

NW Buck Rd.

Plum Creek

NW Hickock Rd.

NE TOWNSHIP 11 (see page 49)

21 72 378 380 381 388 384 387 386 379 378 375 389 388 HH

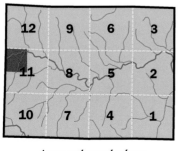

Area enlarged above

TOWNSHIP 11

[Mirabile, NW]

N
W   E
S

Miles

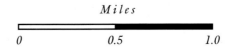

0   0.5   1.0

SE TOWNSHIP 12 (see page 41)

3

| John L. Owen 8-23-36 | John Carill 11-14-36 | John Whitmer 11-14-36 | | Jothan Maynard 2-2-37 | Jothan Maynard 2-2-37 | John Corrill 6-22-36 | Joseph Smith Jr. 9-8-36 | George Morey 2-22-37 | | | William W. Phelps 11-3-36 |

367 · 32 · Sheep Creek

Jacob Whitmer 11-14-36 | John Carill 11-14-36 | John Whitmer 11-14-36 | Abel M. Sargent 1-30-37 | Jothan Maynard 2-2-37 | Jothan Maynard 2-2-37 | John Corrill 6-22-36 | Joseph Smith Jr. 9-8-36 | Uriah B. Lowell 11-18-36 | Levi Jackman 11-16-36 | David Judy 6-24-37 | William W. Phelps 11-3-36

2 **1**

Alvah L. Tippets 12-5-36 | Alvah L. Tippets 12-5-36 | Charles W. Hubbard 1-27-37 | Charles W. Hubbard 1-27-37 | Thomas B. Marsh 1-12-37 | Hiram Smith 6-3-36 | Benjamin Benson 1-31-37 | Isaac Moreley 2-8-37 | Hiram Smith 6-3-36 | Hiram Smith 6-3-36 | Hiram Smith 6-3-36 | W

Shoal Creek

Alvah L. Tippets 12-5-36 | Alvah L. Tippets 12-5-36 | Alvah Benson 2-16-36 | George W. Harris 9-9-36 | Alexander Whiteside 1-12-37 | Hiram Smith 6-3-36 | Benjamin Benson 1-31-37 | Isaac Moreley 2-8-37 | Hiram Smith 6-3-36 | Hiram Smith 6-3-36 | Hiram Smith 6-3-36

NW Willow Dr. · 378 · 368 · 372

William Smith 6-3-37 | Samuel Musick 6-3-37 | Thomas B. Marsh 6-3-37 | Justus Morse 2-1-37 | Burr Riggs 2-9-37 | William W. Phelps 1-31-37 | Squire Bozorth 1-20-37 | Thomas B. Marsh 1-12-37 | Hiram Smith 5-3-36 | Edward Partridge 9-8-36 | Alanson Brown 2-20-37 | George Walter 8-29-36

William Smith 6-3-37 | Alanson Ripley 6-3-37 | Thomas B. Marsh 6-3-37 | Justus Morse 2-1-37 | Ira Clothier 2-1-37 | William W. Phelps 1-31-37 | Squire Bozorth 1-20-37 | Uriah B. Powell 2-13-37 | Hiram Smith 5-3-36 | Edward Partridge 9-8-36 | | George Walter 8-29-36

NW Manson

377 · NW Kerr Dr. · Kerr · 369 · **11** · 369 · **12**

10

Uriah Curtis 1-30-37 | William W. Phelps 8-8-36 | William W. Phelps 8-8-36 | William W. Phelps 8-8-36 | William W. Phelps 8-8-36 | William W. Phelps 8-8-36 | William W. Phelps 11-14-36 | Thomas B. Marsh 2-1-37 | Hiram Smith 9-8-36 | Titus Billings 2-13-37 | John Clemmson 2-13-37 | Samuel Billings 2-13-37

D

Abel M. Sargent 1-30-37 | William W. Phelps 8-8-36 | William W. Phelps 8-8-36 | William W. Phelps 8-8-36 | William W. Phelps 8-8-36 | William W. Phelps 8-8-36 | William W. Phelps 11-14-36 | Thomas B Marsh 2-1-37 | Hiram Smith 9-8-36 | Horace Cowen 2-15-37 | John Clemmson 2-13-37 | John Murdock 7-25-37

375 · 371 · 372

Squire Bozorth 1-20-37 | John Whitmer 1-13-37 | John Whitmer 8-8-36 | John Whitmer 8-8-36 | John Whitmer 8-8-36 | John Whitmer 8-8-36 | John Whitmer 11-14-36 | John Daley 5-29-37 | John Daley 5-29-37 | George M. Hinkel 5-16-37 | George Walter 8-29-36 | George Walter 8-29-36

Far West · 370 · NW Far West Dr. · 370

Squire Bozorth 1-20-37 | John Whitmer 1-13-37 | John Whitmer 8-8-36 | John Whitmer 8-8-36 | John Whitmer 8-8-36 | John Whitmer 8-8-36 | John Whitmer 11-14-36 | John Daley 5-29-37 | John Daley 5-29-37 | Zarah S. Cole 12-28-36 | George Walter 8-29-36 | George Walter 8-29-36

376 · **15** · **14** · Goose Creek · **13** · 358

John Bozorth 1-28-37 | Uriah Curtis 1-26-36 | John Whitmer 1-31-37 | William W. Phelps 11-14-36 | John Whitmer 11-14-36 | Burr Riggs 2-13-37 | John Whitmer 1-31-37 | John Whitmer 12-7-36 | Samuel Musick 8-19-36 | Cyrus Daniels 8-12-36 | James H. Rollins 9-9-36 | John Daley 5-29-37

373

John Bozorth 1-28-37 | Uriah Curtis 1-26-36 | John Whitmer 1-31-37 | William W. Phelps 11-14-36 | John Whitmer 11-14-36 | Burr Riggs 2-13-37 | John Whitmer 1-31-37 | Samuel Musick 8-19-36 | Joseph B. Hawks 11-26-36 | Cyrus Daniels 8-12-36 | John Daley 7-25-37 | Calvin Beebe 7-25-37

NW TOWNSHIP 11 (see page 48) · *NW TOWNSHIP 8 (see page 50)*

SE TOWNSHIP 11 (see page 57)

TOWNSHIP 11

[Mirabile, NE]

N
W — E
S

Miles

0   0.5   1.0

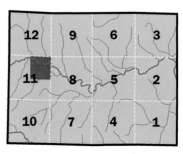

12	9	6	3
11	8	5	2
10	7	4	1

Area enlarged above

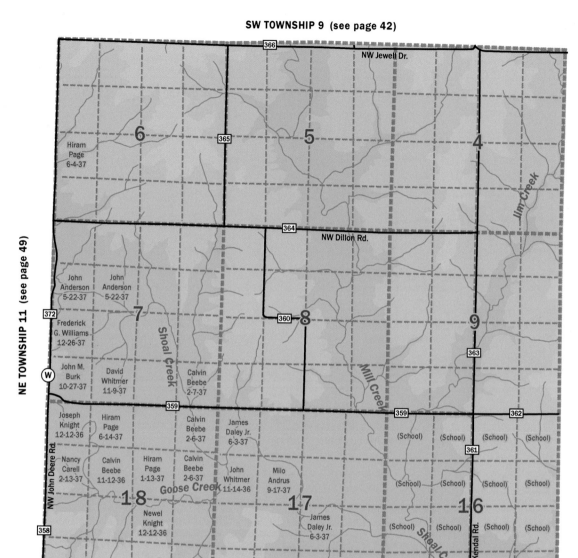

SW TOWNSHIP 9 (see page 42)

366

NW Jewell Dr.

6

Hiram
Page
6-4-37

365

5

4

Jim Creek

NE TOWNSHIP 11 (see page 49)

NE TOWNSHIP 8 (see page 51)

364

NW Dillon Rd.

John
Anderson
5-22-37

John
Anderson
5-22-37

372

7

Frederick
G. Williams
12-26-37

Shoal Creek

360

8

9

363

W

John M.
Burk
10-27-37

David
Whitmer
11-9-37

Calvin
Beebe
2-7-37

Mill Creek

359

359

362

361

Joseph
Knight
12-12-36

Hiram
Page
6-14-37

Calvin
Beebe
2-6-37

James
Daley Jr.
6-3-37

(School)

(School)

(School)

(School)

NW John Deere Rd.

Nancy
Carell
2-13-37

Calvin
Beebe
11-12-36

Hiram
Page
1-13-37

Calvin
Beebe
2-6-37

John
Whitmer
11-14-36

Milo
Andrus
9-17-37

(School)

(School)

(School)

(School)

Goose Creek

18

17

16

358

Newel
Knight
12-12-36

James
Daley Jr.
6-3-37

(School)

(School)

NE Kendal Rd.

(School)

(School)

Shoal Creek

356

(School)

(School)

(School)

361

SW TOWNSHIP 8 (see page 58)

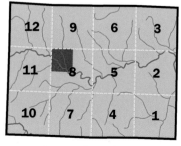

12	9	6	3
11	8	5	2
10	7	4	1

Area enlarged above

TOWNSHIP 8

[Kingston, NW]

Miles

0   0.5   1.0

N

W   E

S

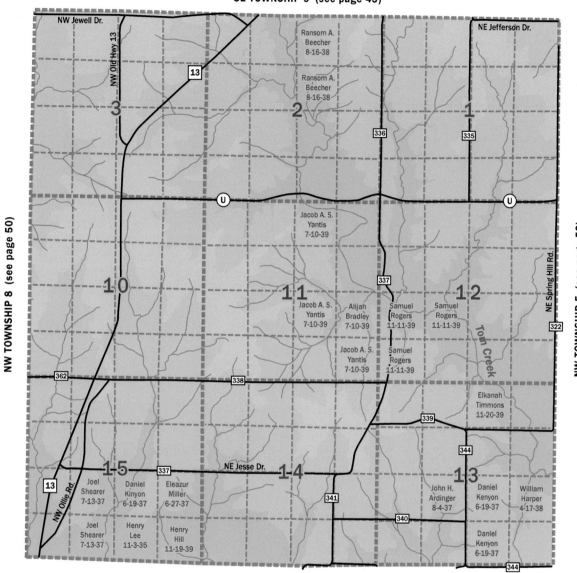

SE TOWNSHIP 9 (see page 43)

NW Jewell Dr.

NE Jefferson Dr.

NW Old Hwy 13

13

Ransom A.
Beecher
8-16-38

3

Ransom A.
Beecher
8-16-38

2

1

336

335

U

U

NW TOWNSHIP 8 (see page 50)

Jacob A. S.
Yantis
7-10-39

337

10

11

Jacob A. S.
Yantis
7-10-39

Alijah
Bradley
7-10-39

Samuel
Rogers
11-11-39

Samuel
Rogers
11-11-39

12

NE Spring Hill Rd.

NW TOWNSHIP 5 (see page 52)

Town Creek

322

Jacob A. S.
Yantis
7-10-39

Samuel
Rogers
11-11-39

362

338

Elkanah
Timmons
11-20-39

339

344

15

337

NE Jesse Dr.

14

13

341

Joel
Shearer
7-13-37

Daniel
Kinyon
6-19-37

Eleazur
Miller
6-27-37

John H.
Ardinger
8-4-37

Daniel
Kenyon
6-19-37

William
Harper
4-17-38

13

NW Ollie Rd.

Joel
Shearer
7-13-37

Henry
Lee
11-3-35

Henry
Hill
11-19-39

340

Daniel
Kenyon
6-19-37

344

SE TOWNSHIP 8 (see page 59)

TOWNSHIP 8

[Kingston, NE]

N
W   E
S

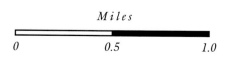

Miles

0   0.5   1.0

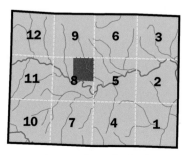

12	9	6	3
11	8	5	2
10	7	4	1

Area enlarged above

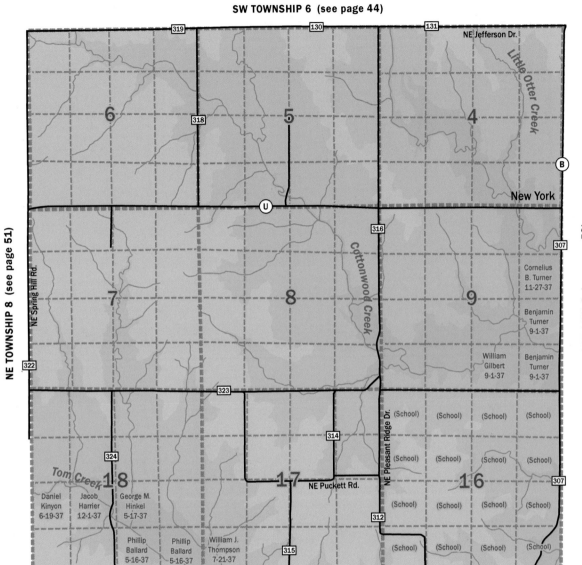

SW TOWNSHIP 6 (see page 44)

NE Jefferson Dr.

Little Otter Creek

6   5   4

B

New York

U

NE Spring Hill Rd.

NE TOWNSHIP 8 (see page 51)

NE TOWNSHIP 5 (see page 53)

Cottonwood Creek

7   8   9

Cornelius
B. Turner
11-27-37

Benjamin
Turner
9-1-37

William   Benjamin
Gilbert   Turner
9-1-37   9-1-37

NE Pleasant Ridge Dr.

(School)   (School)   (School)   (School)

(School)   (School)   (School)   (School)

Tom Creek   18

NE Puckett Rd.   17   16

Daniel   Jacob   George M.
Kinyon   Harrier   Hinkel
6-19-37   12-1-37   5-17-37

(School)   (School)   (School)   (School)

Phillip   Phillip   William J.
Ballard   Ballard   Thompson
5-16-37   5-16-37   7-21-37

(School)   (School)   (School)   (School)

SW TOWNSHIP 5 (see page 60)

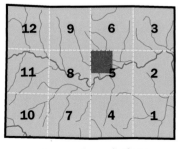

12	9	6	3
11	8	5	2
10	7	4	1

Area enlarged above

TOWNSHIP 5

[New York, NW]

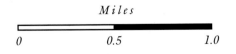

Miles

0   0.5   1.0

N
W   E
S

SE TOWNSHIP 6 (see page 45)

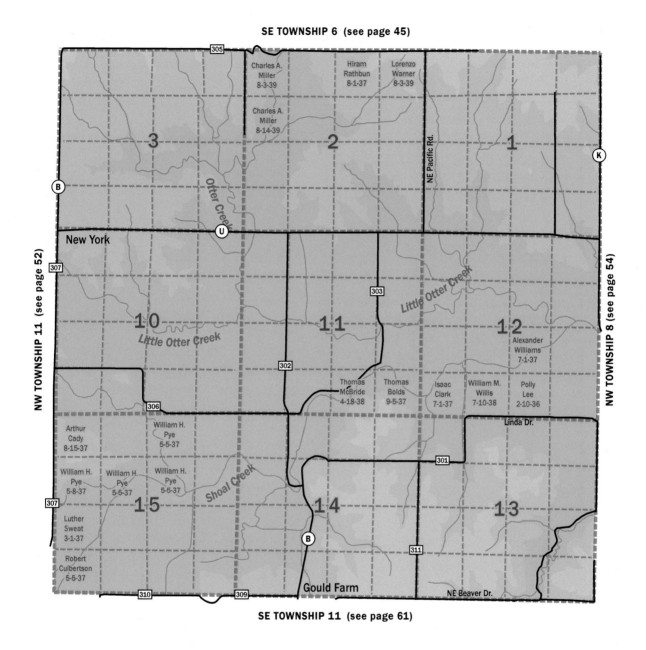

SE TOWNSHIP 11 (see page 61)

TOWNSHIP 5

[New York, NE]

Miles

0   0.5   1.0

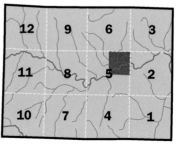

Area enlarged above

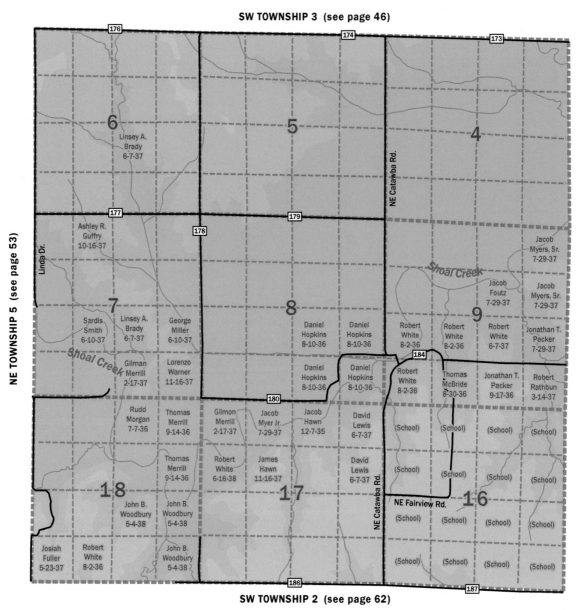

SW TOWNSHIP 3 (see page 46)

NE TOWNSHIP 5 (see page 53)

NE TOWNSHIP 2 (see page 55)

176 | 174 | 173

6

Linsey A. Brady
6-7-37

5

4

NE Catawba Rd.

177 | 178 | 179

Ashley R. Guffry
10-16-37

Jacob Myers, Sr.
7-29-37

Linda Dr.

Shoal Creek

Jacob Foutz
7-29-37

Jacob Myers, Sr.
7-29-37

7

8

9

Sardis Smith
6-10-37

Linsey A. Brady
6-7-37

George Miller
6-10-37

Daniel Hopkins
8-10-36

Daniel Hopkins
8-10-36

Robert White
8-2-36

Robert White
8-2-36

Robert White
6-7-37

Jonathan T. Packer
7-29-37

Shoal Creek

Gilman Merrill
2-17-37

Lorenzo Warner
11-16-37

Daniel Hopkins
8-10-36

Daniel Hopkins
8-10-36

Robert White
8-2-36

184

Thomas McBride
8-30-36

Jonathan T. Packer
9-17-36

Robert Rathbun
3-14-37

180

Rudd Morgan
7-7-36

Thomas Merrill
9-14-36

Gilmon Merrill
2-17-37

Jacob Myer Jr.
7-29-37

Jacob Hawn
12-7-35

David Lewis
6-7-37

(School)

(School)

(School)

(School)

Thomas Merrill
9-14-36

Robert White
6-16-38

James Hawn
11-16-37

David Lewis
6-7-37

(School)

(School)

(School)

(School)

18

17

16

John B. Woodbury
5-4-38

John B. Woodbury
5-4-38

NE Catawba Rd.

NE Fairview Rd.

(School)

(School)

(School)

(School)

Josiah Fuller
5-23-37

Robert White
8-2-36

John B. Woodbury
5-4-38

(School)

(School)

(School)

(School)

186 | 187

SW TOWNSHIP 2 (see page 62)

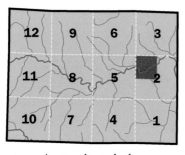

12	9	6	3
11	8	5	2
10	7	4	1

Area enlarged above

TOWNSHIP 2

[Fairview, NW]

Miles

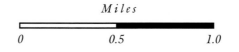

0   0.5   1.0

N
W   E
S

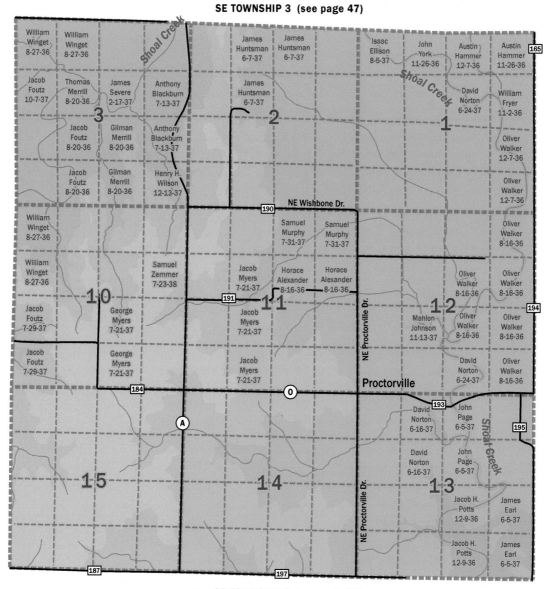

SE TOWNSHIP 3 (see page 47)

SE TOWNSHIP 2 (see page 63)

TOWNSHIP 2

[Fairview, NE]

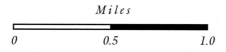

Miles

0   0.5   1.0

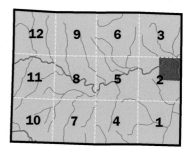

Area enlarged above

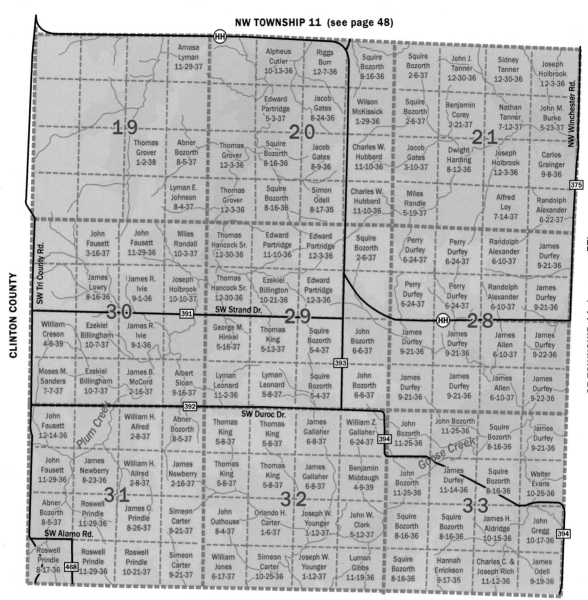

NW TOWNSHIP 11 (see page 48)

Amasa Lyman 11-29-37

Alpheus Cutler 10-13-36

Riggs Burr 12-7-36

Squire Bozorth 8-16-36

Squire Bozorth 2-6-37

John J. Tanner 12-30-36

Sidney Tanner 12-30-36

Joseph Holbrook 12-3-36

19

Edward Partridge 5-3-37

Jacob Gates 8-24-36

Wilson McKissick 1-29-36

Squire Bozorth 2-6-37

Benjamin Corey 2-21-37

Nathan Tanner 7-12-37

John M. Burke 5-23-37

Thomas Grover 1-2-38

Abner Bozorth 8-5-37

Thomas Grover 12-3-36

Squire Bozorth 8-16-36

Jacob Gates 8-9-36

Charles W. Hubbard 11-10-36

Jacob Gates 3-10-37

Dwight Harding 8-12-36

21

Joseph Holbrook 12-3-36

Carlos Grainger 9-8-36

Lyman E. Johnson 8-4-37

Thomas Grover 12-3-36

Squire Bozorth 8-16-36

Simon Odell 8-17-35

Charles W. Hubbard 11-10-36

Miles Randle 5-19-37

Alfred Loy 7-14-37

Randolph Alexander 6-22-37

20

John Fausett 3-16-37

John Fausett 11-29-36

Miles Randall 10-3-37

Thomas Hancock Sr. 12-30-36

Edward Partridge 11-10-36

Edward Partridge 12-3-36

Squire Bozorth 2-6-37

Perry Durfey 6-24-37

Perry Durfey 6-24-37

Randolph Alexander 6-10-37

James Durfey 9-21-36

James Lowry 8-16-34

James R. Ivie 9-1-36

Joseph Holbrook 10-1-37

Thomas Hancock Sr. 12-30-36

Ezekiel Billington 10-21-36

Edward Partridge 12-3-36

Perry Durfey 6-24-37

Perry Durfey 6-24-37

Randolph Alexander 6-10-37

James Durfey 9-21-36

30

SW Strand Dr.

29

28

William Creson 4-6-39

Ezekiel Billingham 10-7-37

James R. Ivie 9-1-36

George M. Hinkel 5-16-37

Thomas King 5-13-37

Squire Bozorth 5-4-37

John Bozorth 6-6-37

James Durfey 9-21-36

James Durfey 9-21-36

James Allen 6-10-37

James Durfey 9-22-36

Moses M. Sanders 7-7-37

Ezekiel Billingham 10-7-37

James B. McCord 2-16-37

Albert Sloan 9-16-37

Lyman Leonard 11-2-36

Lyman Leonard 5-8-37

Squire Bozorth 5-4-37

John Bozorth 6-6-37

James Durfey 9-21-36

James Durfey 9-21-36

James Allen 6-10-37

James Durfey 9-22-36

SW Duroc Dr.

John Fausett 12-14-36

William H. Allred 2-8-37

Abner Bozorth 8-5-37

Thomas King 5-8-37

Thomas King 5-8-37

James Gallaher 6-8-37

William Z. Gallaher 6-24-37

John Bozorth 11-25-36

John Bozorth 11-25-36

Squire Bozorth 8-16-36

James Durfey 9-21-36

John Fausett 11-29-36

James Newberry 8-23-36

William H. Allred 2-8-37

James Newberry 2-16-37

Thomas King 5-8-37

Thomas King 5-8-37

James Gallaher 6-8-37

Benjamin Middaugh 4-9-39

John Bozorth 11-25-36

James Durfey 11-14-36

Squire Bozorth 8-16-36

Walter Evans 10-25-36

31

32

33

Abner Bozorth 8-5-37

Roswell Prindle 11-29-36

James O. Prindle 8-26-37

Simeon Carter 9-21-37

John Outhouse 8-4-37

Orlando H. Carter 1-6-37

Joseph W. Younger 1-12-37

John W. Clark 5-12-37

Squire Bozorth 8-16-36

Squire Bozorth 8-16-36

James H. Aldridge 10-15-36

John Gregg 10-17-36

SW Alamo Rd.

Roswell Prindle 8-17-36

Roswell Prindle 11-29-36

Roswell Prindle 10-21-37

Simeon Carter 9-21-37

William Jones 6-17-37

Simeon Carter 10-25-36

Joseph W. Younger 1-12-37

Luman Gibbs 11-19-36

Squire Bozorth 8-16-36

Hannah Errickson 9-17-35

Charles C. & Joseph Rich 11-12-36

James Odell 9-19-36

CLINTON COUNTY

SW Tri County Rd.

Plum Creek

Goose Creek

NW Winchester Rd.

SE TOWNSHIP 11 (see page 57)

NW TOWNSHIP 10 (see page 64)

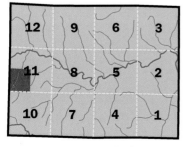

12	9	6	3
11	8	5	2
10	7	4	1

Area enlarged above

TOWNSHIP 11

[Mirabile, SW]

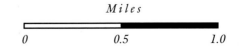

Miles

0   0.5   1.0

N
W   E
S

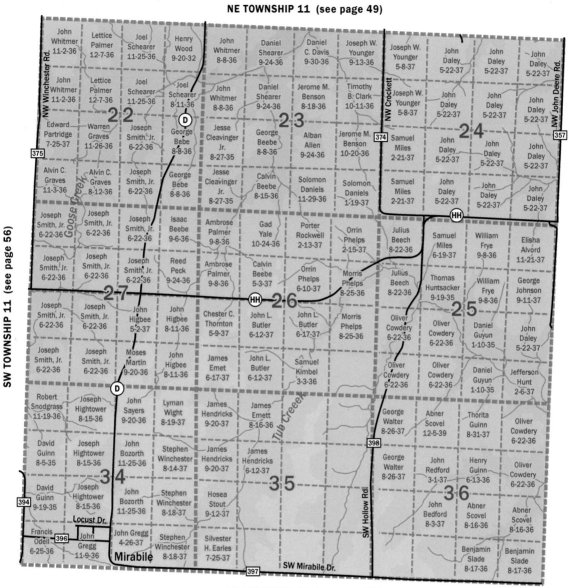

NE TOWNSHIP 11 (see page 49)

Section 22
- John Whitmer 11-2-36
- Lettice Palmer 12-7-36
- Joel Schearer 11-25-36
- Henry Wood 9-20-32
- John Whitmer 11-2-36
- Lettice Palmer 12-7-36
- Joel Schearer 11-25-36
- Joel Schearer 8-11-36
- Edward Partridge 7-25-37
- Warren Graves 11-26-36
- Joseph Smith, Jr. 6-22-36
- George Bebe 8-8-36
- Alvin C. Graves 11-3-36
- Alvin C. Graves 8-12-36
- Joseph Smith, Jr. 6-22-36
- George Bebe 8-8-36

Section 23
- John Whitmer 8-8-36
- Daniel Shearer 9-24-36
- Daniel C. Davis 9-30-36
- Joseph W. Younger 9-13-36
- John Whitmer 8-8-36
- Daniel Shearer 9-24-36
- Jerome M. Benson 8-18-36
- Timothy B. Clark 10-11-36
- Jesse Cleavinger Jr. 8-27-35
- George Beebe 8-8-36
- Alban Allen 9-24-36
- Jerome M. Benson 10-20-36
- Jesse Cleavinger Jr. 8-27-35
- Calvin Beebe 8-15-36
- Solomon Daniels 11-29-36
- Solomon Daniels 1-19-37

Section 24
- Joseph W. Younger 5-8-37
- John Daley 5-22-37
- John Daley 5-22-37
- John Daley 5-22-37
- Joseph W. Younger 5-8-37
- John Daley 5-22-37
- John Daley 5-22-37
- John Daley 5-22-37
- Samuel Miles 2-21-37
- John Daley 5-22-37
- John Daley 5-22-37
- John Daley 5-22-37
- Samuel Miles 2-21-37
- John Daley 5-22-37
- John Daley 5-22-37
- John Daley 5-22-37

Section 27
- Joseph Smith, Jr. 6-22-36
- Joseph Smith, Jr. 6-22-36
- Joseph Smith, Jr. 6-22-36
- Isaac Beebe 9-6-36
- Joseph Smith, Jr. 6-22-36
- Joseph Smith, Jr. 6-22-36
- Joseph Smith, Jr. 6-22-36
- Reed Peck 9-24-36
- Joseph Smith, Jr. 6-22-36
- Joseph Smith, Jr. 6-22-36
- John Higbee 5-2-37
- John Higbee 8-11-36
- Joseph Smith, Jr. 6-22-36
- Joseph Smith, Jr. 6-22-36
- Moses Martin 9-20-36
- John Higbee 8-11-36

Section 26
- Ambrose Palmer 9-8-36
- Gad Yale 10-24-36
- Porter Rockwell 2-13-37
- Orrin Phelps 2-15-37
- Ambrose Palmer 9-8-36
- Calvin Beebe 5-3-37
- Orrin Phelps 6-10-37
- Morris Phelps 8-25-36
- Chester C. Thornton 5-9-37
- John L. Butler 6-12-37
- John L. Butler 6-17-37
- Morris Phelps 8-25-36
- James Emet 6-17-37
- John L. Butler 6-12-37
- Samuel Kimbel 3-3-36

Section 25
- Julius Beech 8-22-36
- Samuel Miles 6-19-37
- William Frye 9-8-36
- Elisha Alvord 11-21-37
- Julius Beech 8-22-36
- Thomas Huntsacker 9-19-35
- William Frye 9-8-36
- George Johnson 9-11-37
- Oliver Cowdery 6-22-36
- Oliver Cowdery 6-22-36
- Daniel Guyun 1-10-35
- John Daley 5-22-37
- Oliver Cowdery 6-22-36
- Oliver Cowdery 6-22-36
- Daniel Guyun 1-10-35
- Jefferson Hunt 2-6-37

Section 34
- Robert Snodgrass 11-19-36
- Joseph Hightower 8-15-36
- John Sayers 9-20-36
- Lyman Wight 8-19-37
- David Guinn 8-5-35
- Joseph Hightower 8-15-36
- John Bozorth 11-25-36
- Stephen Winchester 8-14-37
- David Guinn 9-19-35
- Joseph Hightower 8-15-36
- John Bozorth 11-25-36
- Stephen Winchester 8-18-37
- Francis Odell 6-25-36
- John Gregg 11-9-36
- John Gregg 4-26-37
- Stephen Winchester 8-18-37

Section 35
- James Hendricks 9-20-37
- James Emett 8-16-36
- James Hendricks 9-20-37
- James Hendricks 6-12-37
- Hosea Stout 9-12-36
- Silvester H. Earles 7-25-37

Section 36
- George Walter 8-26-37
- Abner Scovel 12-5-39
- Thorita Guinn 8-31-37
- Oliver Cowdery 6-22-36
- George Walter 8-26-37
- John Redford 3-1-37
- Henry Guinn 6-13-36
- Oliver Cowdery 6-22-36
- John Bedford 8-3-37
- Abner Scovel 8-16-36
- Abner Scovel 8-16-36
- Benjamin Slade 8-17-36
- Benjamin Slade 8-17-36

Mirabile

NE TOWNSHIP 10 (see page 65)

Roads and labels: NW Winchester Rd., NW Crockett, NW John Deere Rd., SW Township 11 (see page 56), SW Township 8 (see page 58), Goose Creek, Tub Creeer, SW Hollow Rd., Locust Dr., SW Mirabile Dr., Mirabile
Route markers: 375, 394, 396, 397, 398, 374, 357

TOWNSHIP 11

[Mirabile, SE]

N
W — E
S

Miles

0   0.5   1.0

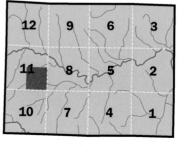

Area enlarged above

12 9 6 3
11 8 5 2
10 7 4 1

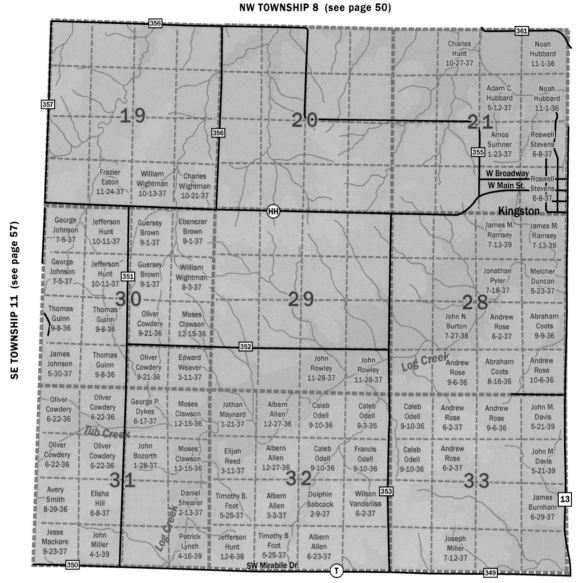

NW TOWNSHIP 8 (see page 50)

356

361

19

357

356

20

355

21

Charles Hunt 10-27-37

Noah Hubbard 11-1-36

Adam C. Hubbard 5-12-37

Noah Hubbard 11-1-36

Amos Sumner 1-23-37

Roswell Stevens 6-8-37

W Broadway
W Main St.

Roswell Stevens 6-8-37

Frazier Eaton 11-24-37

William Wightman 10-13-37

Charles Wightman 10-21-37

HH

Kingston

SE TOWNSHIP 11 (see page 57)

SE TOWNSHIP 8 (see page 59)

George Johnson 7-5-37

Jefferson Hunt 10-11-37

Guersey Brown 9-1-37

Ebenezer Brown 9-1-37

James M. Ramsey 7-13-39

James M. Ramsey 7-13-39

George Johnson 7-5-37

Jefferson Hunt 10-11-37

351

Guersey Brown 9-1-37

William Wightman 8-3-37

Jonathan Pyler 7-18-37

Melcher Duncan 5-23-37

30

29

28

Thomas Guinn 9-8-36

Thomas Guinn 9-8-36

Oliver Cowdery 9-21-36

Moses Clawson 12-15-36

John N. Burton 7-27-38

Andrew Rose 6-2-37

Abraham Coots 9-9-36

James Johnson 5-30-37

Thomas Guinn 9-8-36

Oliver Cowdery 9-21-36

Edward Weaver 3-11-37

352

John Rowley 11-28-37

John Rowley 11-28-37

Log Creek

Andrew Rose 9-6-36

Abraham Coots 8-16-36

Andrew Rose 10-6-36

Oliver Cowdery 6-22-36

Oliver Cowdery 6-22-36

George P. Dykes 6-17-37

Moses Clawson 12-15-36

Jothan Maynard 1-21-37

Albern Allen 12-27-36

Caleb Odell 9-10-36

Caleb Odell 9-3-35

Caleb Odell 9-10-36

Andrew Rose 6-2-37

Andrew Rose 9-6-36

John M. Davis 5-21-39

Tub Creek

Oliver Cowdery 6-22-36

Oliver Cowdery 6-22-36

John Bozorth 1-28-37

Moses Clawson 12-15-36

Elijah Reed 3-11-37

Albern Allen 12-27-36

Caleb Odell 9-10-36

Francis Odell 9-10-36

Caleb Odell 9-10-36

Andrew Rose 6-2-37

John M. Davis 5-21-39

31

32

353

33

Avery Smith 8-29-36

Elisha Hill 6-8-37

Daniel Shearer 2-13-37

Timothy B. Foot 5-25-37

Albern Allen 3-3-37

Dolphin Babcock 2-9-37

Wilson Vanderliss 6-2-37

James Burnham 6-29-37

13

Log Creek

Jesse Mackare 9-23-37

John Miller 4-1-39

Patrick Lynch 4-16-39

Jefferson Hunt 12-6-36

Timothy B. Foot 5-25-37

Albern Allen 6-23-37

Joseph Miller 7-12-37

350

SW Mirabile Dr.

T

349

NW TOWNSHIP 7 (see page 66)

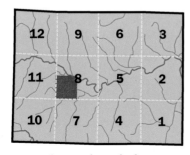

12	9	6	3
11	8	5	2
10	7	4	1

Area enlarged above

TOWNSHIP 8

[Kingston, SW]

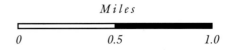

Miles

0   0.5   1.0

N
W   E
S

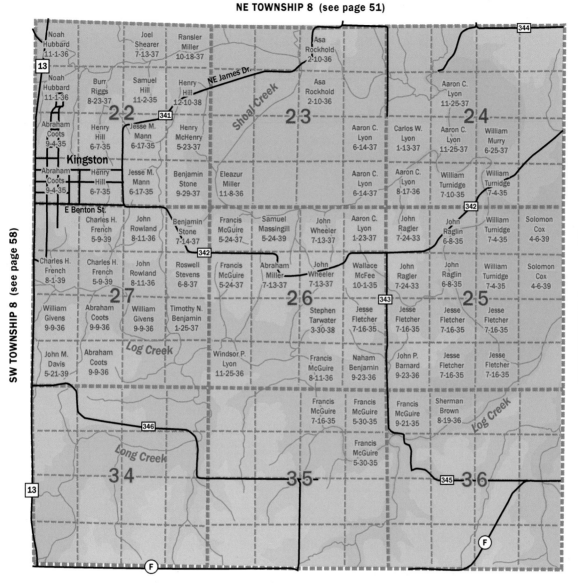

NE TOWNSHIP 8 (see page 51)

SW TOWNSHIP 8 (see page 58)

SW TOWNSHIP 5 (see page 60)

Noah Hubbard 11-1-36	Joel Shearer 7-13-37	Ransler Miller 10-18-37		Asa Rockhold 2-10-36		Aaron C. Lyon 11-25-37	
Noah Hubbard 11-1-36	Burr Riggs 8-23-37	Samuel Hill 11-2-35	Henry Hill 12-10-38	Asa Rockhold 2-10-36			
Abraham Coots 9-4-35	Henry Hill 6-7-35	Jesse M. Mann 6-17-35	Henry McHenry 5-23-37		Aaron C. Lyon 6-14-37	Carlos W. Lyon 1-13-37	Aaron C. Lyon 11-25-37	William Murry 6-25-37
Kingston							
Abraham Coots 9-4-35	Henry Hill 6-7-35	Jesse M. Mann 6-17-35	Benjamin Stone 9-29-37	Eleazur Miller 11-8-36	Aaron C. Lyon 6-14-37	Aaron C. Lyon 8-17-36	William Turnidge 7-10-35	William Turnidge 7-4-35

22   **23**   **24**

E Benton St.

| Charles H. French 5-9-39 | John Rowland 8-11-36 | Benjamin Stone 7-14-37 | Francis McGuire 5-24-37 | Samuel Massingill 5-24-39 | John Wheeler 7-13-37 | Aaron C. Lyon 1-23-37 | John Ragler 7-24-33 | John Raglin 6-8-35 | William Turnidge 7-4-35 | Solomon Cox 4-6-39 |
| Charles H. French 8-1-39 | Charles H. French 5-9-39 | John Rowland 8-11-36 | Roswell Stevens 6-8-37 | Francis McGuire 5-24-37 | Abraham Miller 7-13-37 | John Wheeler 7-13-37 | Wallace McFee 10-1-35 | John Ragler 7-24-33 | John Raglin 6-8-35 | William Turnidge 7-4-35 | Solomon Cox 4-6-39 |

27   **26**   **25**

William Givens 9-9-36	Abraham Coots 9-9-36	William Givens 9-9-36	Timothy N. Benjamin 1-25-37		Stephen Tarwater 3-30-38	Jesse Fletcher 7-16-35	Jesse Fletcher 7-16-35	Jesse Fletcher 7-16-35	Jesse Fletcher 7-16-35
John M. Davis 5-21-39	Abraham Coots 9-9-36		Windsor P. Lyon 11-25-36	Francis McGuire 8-11-36	Naham Benjamin 9-23-36	John P. Barnard 9-23-36	Jesse Fletcher 7-16-35	Jesse Fletcher 7-16-35
				Francis McGuire 7-16-35	Francis McGuire 5-30-35	Francis McGuire 9-21-35	Sherman Brown 8-19-36
					Francis McGuire 5-30-35		

34   **35**   **36**

NE TOWNSHIP 7 (see page 67)

TOWNSHIP 8

[Kingston, SE]

N
W   E
S

Miles

| 0 | 0.5 | 1.0 |

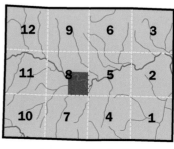

12	9	6	3
11	8	5	2
10	7	4	1

Area enlarged above

NW TOWNSHIP 5 (see page 52)

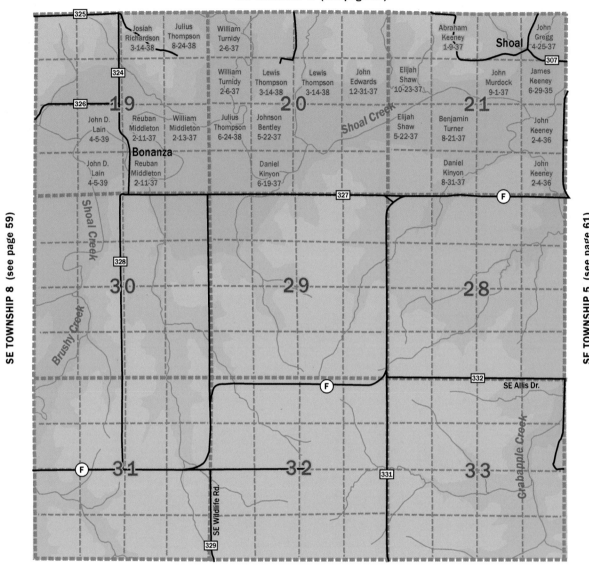

325

Josiah
Richardson
3-14-38

Julius
Thompson
8-24-38

William
Turnidy
2-6-37

Abraham
Keeney
1-9-37

Shoal

John
Gregg
4-25-37

307

324

William
Turnidy
2-6-37

Lewis
Thompson
3-14-38

Lewis
Thompson
3-14-38

John
Edwards
12-31-37

Elijah
Shaw
10-23-37

John
Murdock
9-1-37

James
Keeney
6-29-35

326

19

John D.
Lain
4-5-39

Reuban
Middleton
2-11-37

William
Middleton
2-13-37

Julius
Thompson
6-24-38

Johnson
Bentley
5-22-37

20

Shoal Creek

Elijah
Shaw
5-22-37

21

Benjamin
Turner
8-21-37

John
Keeney
2-4-36

Bonanza

John D.
Lain
4-5-39

Reuban
Middleton
2-11-37

Daniel
Kinyon
6-19-37

Daniel
Kinyon
8-31-37

John
Keeney
2-4-36

327

F

SE TOWNSHIP 8 (see page 59)

Shoal Creek

328

30

Brushy Creek

29

28

SE TOWNSHIP 5 (see page 61)

332

SE Allis Dr.

F

Crabapple Creek

F

31

32

SE Wildlife Rd.

331

33

329

NW TOWNSHIP 4 (see page 68)

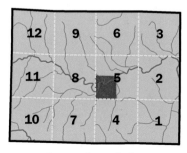

12	9	6	3
11	8	5	2
10	7	4	1

Area enlarged above

TOWNSHIP 5

[New York, SW]

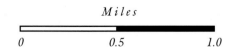

Miles

0   0.5   1.0

N
W   E
S

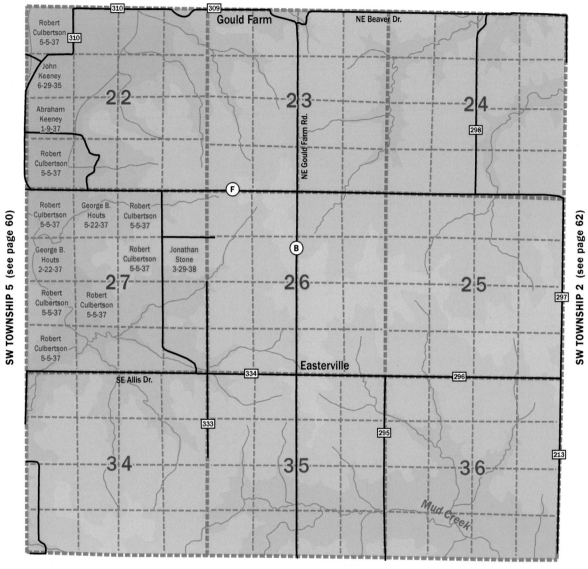

NE TOWNSHIP 5 (see page 53)

Gould Farm

NE Beaver Dr.

Robert Culbertson 5-5-37 [310]

John Keeney 6-29-35

Abraham Keeney 1-9-37

Robert Culbertson 5-5-37

22

23

NE Gould Farm Rd.

24 [298]

SW TOWNSHIP 5 (see page 60)

SW TOWNSHIP 2 (see page 62)

Robert Culbertson 5-5-37

George B. Houts 5-22-37

Robert Culbertson 5-5-37

George B. Houts 2-22-37

Robert Culbertson 5-5-37

Jonathan Stone 3-29-38

Robert Culbertson 5-5-37

Robert Culbertson 5-5-37

Robert Culbertson 5-5-37

27

26

25 [297]

Easterville

SE Allis Dr. [334] [296]

[333]

[295]

34

35

36 [213]

Mud Creek

NE TOWNSHIP 4 (see page 69)

TOWNSHIP 5

[New York, SE]

N
W — E
S

Miles

0   0.5   1.0

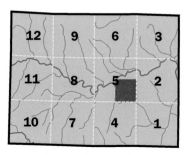

12	9	6	3
11	8	5	2
10	7	4	1

Area enlarged above

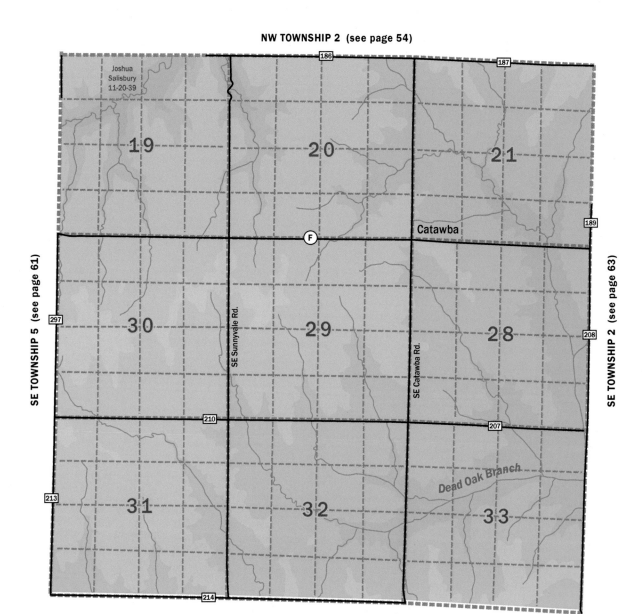

NW TOWNSHIP 2 (see page 54)

186   187

19   20   21

189

Catawba

F

30   29   28

SE Sunnyvale Rd.

SE Catawba Rd.

297   208

210   207

Joshua
Salisbury
11-20-39

SE TOWNSHIP 5 (see page 61)

SE TOWNSHIP 2 (see page 63)

213   Dead Oak Branch

31   32   33

214

NW TOWNSHIP 1 (see page 70)

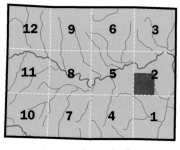

12	9	6	3
11	8	5	2
10	7	4	1

Area enlarged above

TOWNSHIP 2

[Fairview, SW]

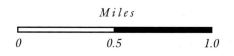

Miles

0   0.5   1.0

N
W   E
S

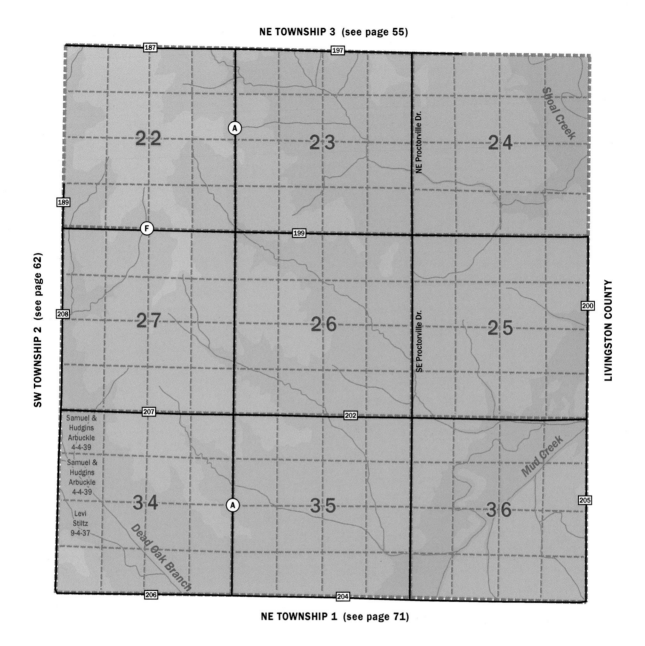

NE TOWNSHIP 3 (see page 55)

187 | 197

22 | 23 | 24

Shoal Creek

NE Proctorville Dr.

A

189

F | 199

SW TOWNSHIP 2 (see page 62)

208

27 | 26 | 25

SE Proctorville Dr.

LIVINGSTON COUNTY

200

207 | 202

Samuel &
Hudgins
Arbuckle
4-4-39

Samuel &
Hudgins
Arbuckle
4-4-39

Mud Creek

205

Levi
Stiltz
9-4-37

34 | A | 35 | 36

Dead Oak Branch

206 | 204

NE TOWNSHIP 1 (see page 71)

TOWNSHIP 2

[Fairview, SE]

N
W · E
S

Miles

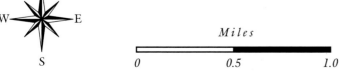

0   0.5   1.0

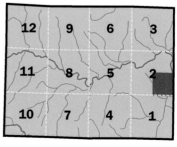

12	9	6	3
11	8	5	2
10	7	4	1

Area enlarged above

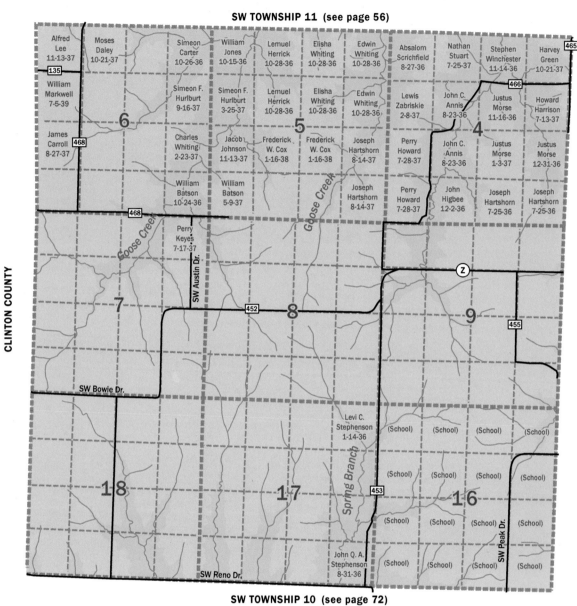

SW TOWNSHIP 11 (see page 56)

6

Alfred Lee 11-13-37
Moses Daley 10-21-37
Simeon Carter 10-26-36
William Jones 10-15-36
Lemuel Herrick 10-28-36
Elisha Whiting 10-28-36
Edwin Whiting 10-28-36
Absalom Scrichfield 8-27-36
Nathan Stuart 7-25-37
Stephen Winchester 11-14-36
Harvey Green 10-21-37

William Markwell 7-5-39
Simeon F. Hurlburt 9-16-37
Simeon F. Hurlburt 3-25-37
Lemuel Herrick 10-28-36
Elisha Whiting 10-28-36
Edwin Whiting 10-28-36
Lewis Zabriskie 2-8-37
John C. Annis 8-23-36
Justus Morse 11-16-36
Howard Harrison 7-13-37

5 **4**

James Carroll 8-27-37
Charles Whiting 2-23-37
Jacob Johnson 11-13-37
Frederick W. Cox 1-16-38
Frederick W. Cox 1-16-38
Joseph Hartshorn 8-14-37
Perry Howard 7-28-37
John C. Annis 8-23-36
Justus Morse 1-3-37
Justus Morse 12-31-36

William Batson 10-24-36
William Batson 5-9-37
Joseph Hartshorn 8-14-37
Perry Howard 7-28-37
John Higbee 12-2-36
Joseph Hartshorn 7-25-36
Joseph Hartshorn 7-25-36

Perry Keyes 7-17-37

7 **8** **9**

Levi C. Stephenson 1-14-36
(School) (School) (School) (School)

18 **17** **16**

(School) (School) (School) (School)

SW Bowie Dr.

(School) (School) (School) (School)

John Q. A. Stephenson 8-31-36
(School) (School) (School) (School)

SW Reno Dr.

SW TOWNSHIP 10 (see page 72)

Goose Creek
Spring Branch
CLINTON COUNTY
SW Austin Dr.
SW Peak Dr.
NE TOWNSHIP 10 (see page 65)

135
468
468
452
453
455
465
466
Z

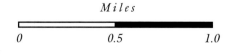

TOWNSHIP 10

[Rockford, NW]

12	9	6	3
11	8	5	2
10	7	4	1

Area enlarged above

Miles

0   0.5   1.0

N
W   E
S

SE TOWNSHIP 11 (see page 57)

SW Mirabile Dr.

SW Duroc Dr.

465

| 397 | 464 | 461 | 463 |

3

2

1

NW TOWNSHIP 10 (see page 64)

NW TOWNSHIP 7 (see page 66)

Harvey Green 11-26-36 | Harvey Green 11-26-36 | Charles C. & Joseph Rich 4-26-37 | Timothy B. Clark 6-12-37 | Timothy B. Clark 6-6-37 | Austin Whitlock 8-26-37 | Wesley Hines 8-26-36 | William L. Butts 7-15-39 | Hiram Abbott 12-3-36

Charles C. & Joseph Rich 4-26-37 | Charles C. & Joseph Rich 4-26-37 | Charles C. & Joseph Rich 4-26-37 | Timothy B. Clark 6-12-37 | Timothy B. Clark 6-6-37 | Austin Whitlock 8-26-37 | Wesley Hines 8-26-36 | Philip Curtis 10-2-38 | Hiram Abbott 2-13-37 | James Allred 9-4-37

Pierce Hawley 9-29-37 | John Larkey 12-7-36 | John Larkey 6-5-37 | Henry Snyder 10-11-36 | Joseph Woods 2-24-34 | Martin C. Allred 11-5-36 | Lewis Turner 9-7-36 | Harris Park 8-12-36 | Charles P. Curtis 8-12-36 | James Allred 8-26-37 | Reuben W. Allred 8-26-37

Pierce Hawley 9-29-37 | Edward Larkey 9-21-36 | George L. Oster 8-30-39 | John Larkey 6-5-37 | Henry Snyder 10-11-36 | Joseph Woods 2-24-34 | Gardner Sherman 9-7-36 | Lewis Turner 9-7-36 | Harris Park 8-12-36 | Charles P. Curtis 8-12-36 | Reuben W. Allred 12-19-37 | Jeremiah Curtis 10-12-37

SW Hollow Dr.

462

Log Creek

Elisha Vorhees 2-17-37 | John Larkey 9-16-36 | John Larkey 9-16-36 | John Larkey 9-21-36 | Anthony Hendricks 8-17-36 | Henry Snyder 10-11-36 | Lewis Turner 11-2-36 | Andrew Whitlock 10-24-36 | James McCord 8-17-36 | Hiram Smith 11-2-36

Z

10

11

12

Charles Stumett Jr. 11-14-37 | Benjamin Jones 4-26-37 | Christopher Cunningham 7-5-36 | Charley Stennet 2-6-37 | Henry Snyder 10-11-36 | Abner Bozorth 7-12-37 | William C. Clark 2-16-37 | Harry Park 8-12-36 | James B. McCord 8-26-36 | Hiram Smith 11-2-36 | Rufus Abbott 5-19-37

SW Houston

SW Peak Dr.

Lindsey A. Brady 7-29-37 | Christopher Cunningham 9-1-36 | Timothy B. Clark 8-18-36 | Richard B. Stennet 12-6-36 | Benjamin Jones 2-26-37 | George Slade 2-16-37 | Aaron Batterick 2-8-37 | Martin C. Allred 10-24-36 | Thomas M. Hines 5-18-39 | Calvin H. Nicholson 8-27-36 | George Walter 8-29-36

Jedediah Owen 7-29-37 | Christopher Cunningham 9-1-36 | Timothy B. Clark 8-18-36 | Moses Morse 9-6-36 | Benjamin Bragg 8-20-36 | Jesse M. Carroll 9-10-36 | Silvester H. Earl 5-16-37 | Hiram Smith 11-2-36 | Calvin H. Nicholson 8-27-36 | George Walter 8-29-36

D

460

Jedediah Owen 12-1-36 | John Cooper 8-18-36 | Landon Rich 11-12-36 | Isaac Odell 8-3-36 | Isaac Odell 7-1-36 | Jesse McCarroll 9-11-36 | Jerome M. Benson 11-28-36 | Isaac Moreley 2-25-37 | Wiley P. Allred 2-21-37 | James Aldrich 10-26-36

SW Peak Dr.

John Cooper 8-8-37 | Landon Rich 4-26-37 | Landon Rich 11-12-36 | Isaac Odell 8-3-36 | Moses Morse 9-16-36 | Lucius H. Fuller 3-16-37 | Lucius H. Fuller 10-4-36 | Isaac Moreley 2-25-37 | Jotham Maynard 2-22-37 | John Loveless 11-26-36

15

14

SW Colt Dr.

13

Solomon Wiscom 7-7-37 | Jedediah Owen 12-1-36 | Walter Selvey 6-23-37 | Walter Selvey 6-23-37 | Roswell Evans 8-10-37 | Roswell Evans 10-14-36 | James Huston 11-5-36 | Francis H. Green 10-31-39 | Walter Selvey 2-15-37 | Israel Duty 9-1-36

John Crowley 10-28-39 | Marcellus McKown 9-22-36 | James Huston 11-5-36 | Francis H. Green 10-31-39 | Israel Duty 4-27-37 | Israel Duty 9-1-36

SE TOWNSHIP 10 (see page 73)

TOWNSHIP 10

[Rockford, NE]

N
W   E
S

Miles

0   0.5   1.0

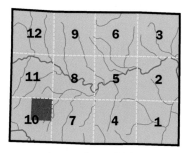

12	9	6	3
11	8	5	2
10	7	4	1

Area enlarged above

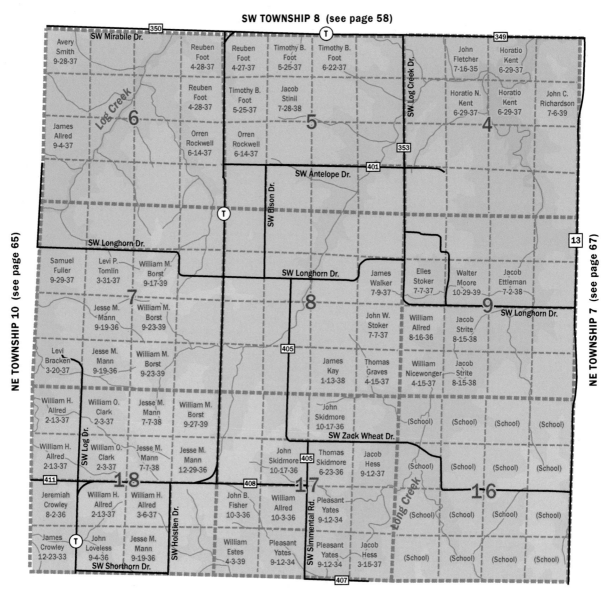

SW TOWNSHIP 8 (see page 58)

SW Mirabile Dr.

350

Avery
Smith
9-28-37

Reuben
Foot
4-28-37

Reuben
Foot
4-27-37

Timothy B.
Foot
5-25-37

Timothy B.
Foot
6-22-37

349

John
Fletcher
7-16-35

Horatio
Kent
6-29-37

Reuben
Foot
4-28-37

Timothy B.
Foot
5-25-37

Jacob
Stinil
7-28-38

Horatio N.
Kent
6-29-37

Horatio
Kent
6-29-37

John C.
Richardson
7-6-39

Log Creek

6

James
Allred
9-4-37

Orren
Rockwell
6-14-37

Orren
Rockwell
6-14-37

5

4

SW Log Creek Dr.

353

401

SW Antelope Dr.

SW Bison Dr.

SW Longhorn Dr.

13

Samuel
Fuller
9-29-37

Levi P.
Tomlin
3-31-37

William M.
Borst
9-17-39

SW Longhorn Dr.

James
Walker
7-9-37

Elles
Stoker
7-7-37

Walter
Moore
10-29-39

Jacob
Ettleman
7-2-38

7

Jesse M.
Mann
9-19-36

William M.
Borst
9-23-39

8

John W.
Stoker
7-7-37

William
Allred
8-16-36

Jacob
Strite
8-15-38

9

SW Longhorn Dr.

Levi
Bracken
3-20-37

Jesse M.
Mann
9-19-36

William M.
Borst
9-23-39

405

James
Kay
1-13-38

Thomas
Graves
4-15-37

William
Nicewonger
4-15-37

Jacob
Strite
8-15-38

William H.
Allred
2-13-37

William O.
Clark
2-3-37

Jesse M.
Mann
7-7-38

William M.
Borst
9-27-39

John
Skidmore
10-17-36

(School)

(School)

(School)

(School)

SW Zack Wheat Dr.

William H.
Allred
2-13-37

SW Log Dr.

William O.
Clark
2-3-37

Jesse M.
Mann
7-7-38

Jesse M.
Mann
12-29-36

John
Skidmore
10-17-36

405

Thomas
Skidmore
6-23-36

Jacob
Hess
9-12-37

(School)

(School)

(School)

(School)

411

1-8

408

1-7

1-6

Jeremiah
Crowley
8-2-36

William H.
Allred
2-13-37

William H.
Allred
3-6-37

SW Holstien Dr.

John B.
Fisher
10-3-36

William
Allred
10-3-36

Pleasant
Yates
9-12-34

SW Simmental Rd.

(School)

(School)

(School)

(School)

Long Creek

James
Crowley
12-23-33

John
Loveless
9-4-36

Jesse M.
Mann
9-19-36

William
Estes
4-3-39

Pleasant
Yates
9-12-34

Pleasant
Yates
9-12-34

Jacob
Hess
3-15-37

(School)

(School)

(School)

(School)

SW Shorthorn Dr.

407

SW TOWNSHIP 7 (see page 74)

NE TOWNSHIP 10 (see page 65)

NE TOWNSHIP 7 (see page 67)

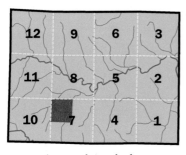

12	9	6	3
11	8	5	2
10	7	4	1

Area enlarged above

TOWNSHIP 7

[Grant, NW]

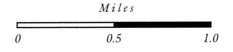

Miles

0   0.5   1.0

N
W   E
S

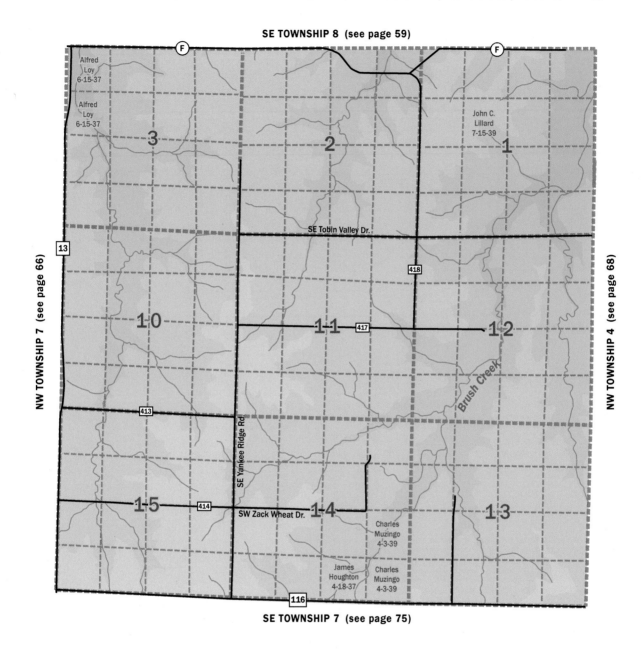

SE TOWNSHIP 8 (see page 59)

Alfred
Loy
6-15-37

Alfred
Loy
6-15-37

3

2

1

John C.
Lillard
7-15-39

NW TOWNSHIP 7 (see page 66)

NW TOWNSHIP 4 (see page 68)

SE Tobin Valley Dr.

10

11

12

Brush Creek

SE Yankee Ridge Rd.

SW Zack Wheat Dr.

15

14

13

Charles
Muzingo
4-3-39

James
Houghton
4-18-37

Charles
Muzingo
4-3-39

SE TOWNSHIP 7 (see page 75)

TOWNSHIP 7

[Grant, NE]

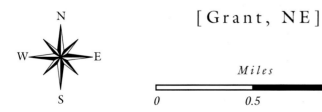

Miles

0   0.5   1.0

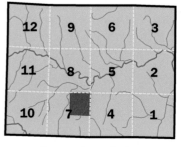

12	9	6	3
11	8	5	2
10	7	4	1

Area enlarged above

SW TOWNSHIP 5 (see page 60)

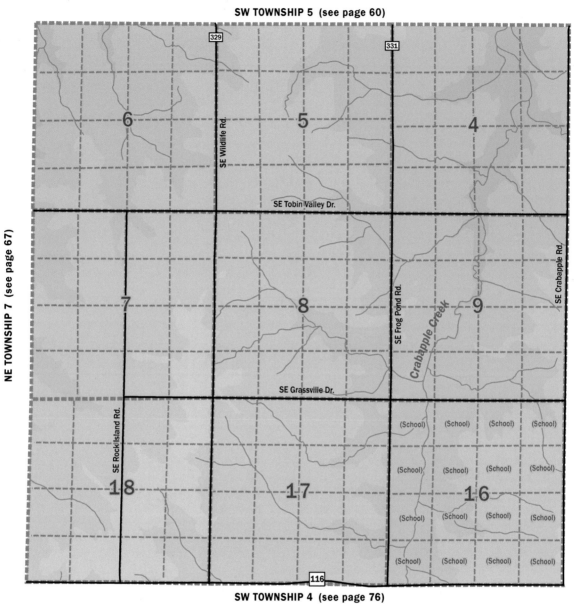

329

331

SE Wildlife Rd.

6

5

4

SE Tobin Valley Dr.

NE TOWNSHIP 7 (see page 67)

NE TOWNSHIP 4 (see page 69)

7

8

SE Frog Pond Rd.

Crabapple Creek

SE Crabapple Rd.

9

SE Grassville Dr.

SE Rock Island Rd.

(School) (School) (School) (School)

(School) (School) (School) (School)

18

17

16

(School) (School) (School) (School)

(School) (School) (School) (School)

116

SW TOWNSHIP 4 (see page 76)

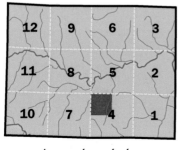

12 9 6 3

11 8 5 2

10 7 4 1

Area enlarged above

TOWNSHIP 4

[Lincoln, NW]

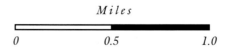

Miles

0   0.5   1.0

N

W E

S

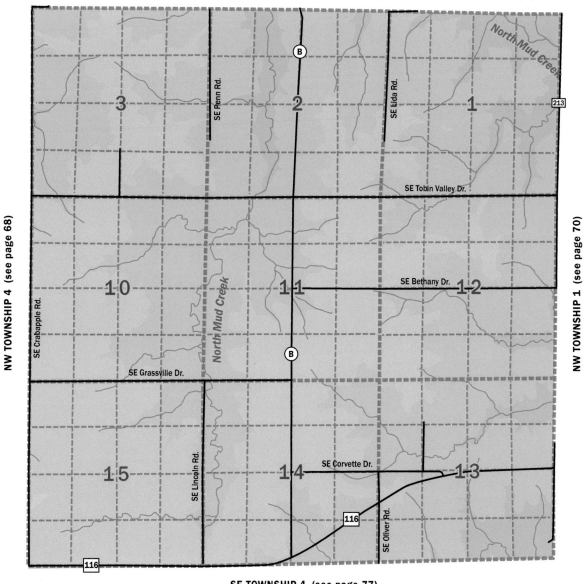

SE TOWNSHIP 5 (see page 61)

North Mud Creek

SE Penn Rd.

SE Lida Rd.

SE Tobin Valley Dr.

NW TOWNSHIP 4 (see page 68)

NW TOWNSHIP 1 (see page 70)

SE Crabapple Rd.

North Mud Creek

SE Bethany Dr.

SE Grassville Dr.

SE Lincoln Rd.

SE Corvette Dr.

SE Oliver Rd.

SE TOWNSHIP 4 (see page 77)

TOWNSHIP 4

[Lincoln, NE]

Miles

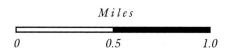

0   0.5   1.0

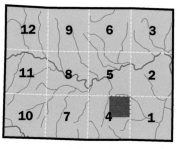

Area enlarged above

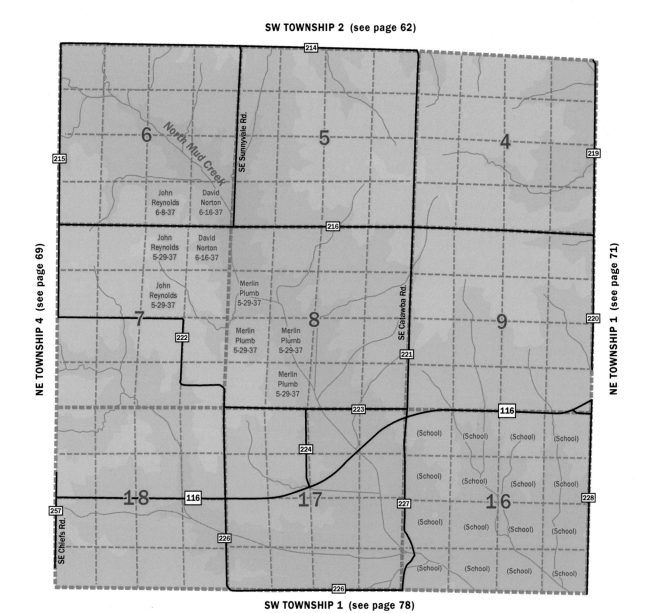

SW TOWNSHIP 2 (see page 62)

214

NE TOWNSHIP 4 (see page 69)

NE TOWNSHIP 1 (see page 71)

6

North Mud Creek

SE Sunnyvale Rd.

5

4

215

219

John
Reynolds
6-8-37

David
Norton
6-16-37

216

John
Reynolds
5-29-37

David
Norton
6-16-37

John
Reynolds
5-29-37

Merlin
Plumb
5-29-37

8

SE Catawba Rd.

9

220

7

222

Merlin
Plumb
5-29-37

Merlin
Plumb
5-29-37

221

Merlin
Plumb
5-29-37

223

116

18

116

17

16

257

SE Chiefs Rd.

224

227

228

(School) (School) (School) (School)

(School) (School) (School) (School)

(School) (School) (School) (School)

(School) (School) (School) (School)

226

226

SW TOWNSHIP 1 (see page 78)

12	9	6	3
11	8	5	2
10	7	4	1

Area enlarged above

TOWNSHIP 1

[Davis, NW]

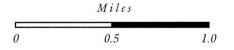

Miles

0   0.5   1.0

N

W — E

S

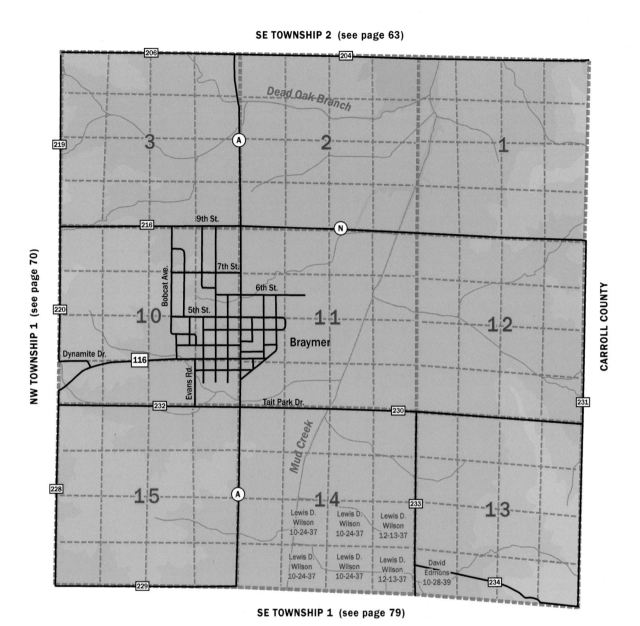

SE TOWNSHIP 2 (see page 63)

SE TOWNSHIP 1 (see page 79)

TOWNSHIP 1

[Davis, NE]

Miles

0   0.5   1.0

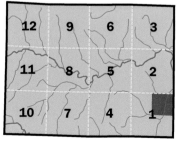

Area enlarged above

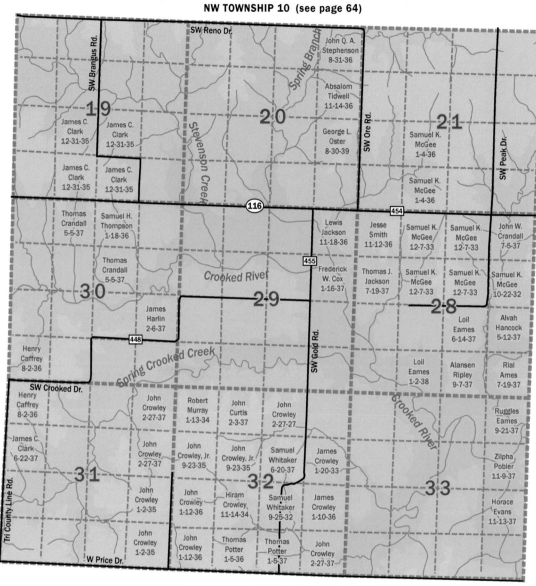

NW TOWNSHIP 10 (see page 64)

SW Reno Dr.

SW Brangus Rd.

Spring Branch

John Q. A. Stephenson
8-31-36

CLINTON COUNTY

19

James C. Clark
12-31-35

James C. Clark
12-31-35

James C. Clark
12-31-35

James C. Clark
12-31-35

Stevenson Creek

20

Absalom Tidwell
11-14-36

George L. Oster
8-30-39

SW Ore Rd.

21

Samuel K. McGee
1-4-36

Samuel K. McGee
1-4-36

SW Peak Dr.

116

454

Thomas Crandall
5-5-37

Samuel H. Thompson
1-18-36

Thomas Crandall
5-5-37

Lewis Jackson
11-18-36

Jesse Smith
11-12-36

Samuel K. McGee
12-7-33

Samuel K. McGee
12-7-33

John W. Crandall
7-5-37

Crooked River

455

30

James Harlin
2-6-37

29

Frederick W. Cox
1-16-37

Thomas J. Jackson
7-19-37

Samuel K. McGee
12-7-33

Samuel K. McGee
12-7-33

Samuel K. McGee
10-22-32

SE TOWNSHIP 10 (see page 73)

448

Henry Caffrey
8-2-36

Spring Crooked Creek

SW Gold Rd.

28

Loil Eames
6-14-37

Alvah Hancock
5-12-37

SW Crooked Dr.

Henry Caffrey
8-2-36

Loil Eames
1-2-38

Alansen Ripley
9-7-37

Rial Ames
7-19-37

James C. Clark
6-22-37

John Crowley
2-27-37

Robert Murray
1-13-34

John Curtis
2-3-37

John Crowley
2-27-27

Crooked River

Ruggles Eames
9-21-37

Tri County Line Rd.

31

John Crowley
2-27-37

John Crowley, Jr.
9-23-35

John Crowley, Jr.
9-23-35

Samuel Whitaker
6-20-37

James Crowley
1-20-33

33

Zilpha Pobler
11-9-37

John Crowley
1-2-35

John Crowley
1-12-36

Hiram Crowley
11-14-34

32

Samuel Whitaker
9-25-32

James Crowley
1-10-36

Horace Evans
11-13-37

John Crowley
1-2-35

W Price Dr.

John Crowley
1-12-36

Thomas Potter
1-5-36

Thomas Potter
1-5-37

John Crowley
2-27-37

RAY COUNTY (area added to Ray in 1839)

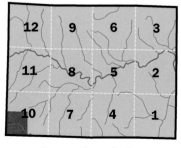

12	9	6	3
11	8	5	2
10	7	4	1

Area enlarged above

TOWNSHIP 10

[Rockford, SW]

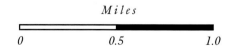

Miles

0   0.5   1.0

N
W   E
S

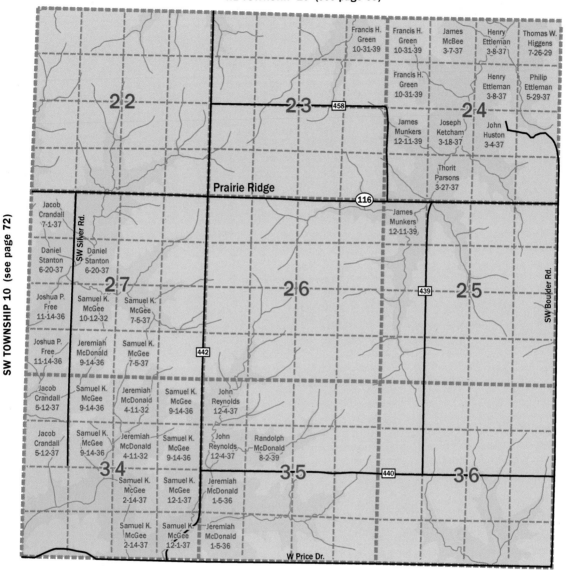

NE TOWNSHIP 10 (see page 65)

SW TOWNSHIP 10 (see page 72)

SW TOWNSHIP 7 (see page 74)

Francis H. Green 10-31-39

Francis H. Green 10-31-39

James McBee 3-7-37

Henry Ettleman 3-8-37

Thomas W. Higgens 7-26-29

22

23

458

Francis H. Green 10-31-39

Henry Ettleman 3-8-37

Philip Ettleman 5-29-37

24

James Munkers 12-11-39

Joseph Ketcham 3-18-37

John Huston 3-4-37

Thorit Parsons 3-27-37

Prairie Ridge

116

James Munkers 12-11-39

Jacob Crandall 7-1-37

Daniel Stanton 6-20-37

Daniel Stanton 6-20-37

SW Silver Rd.

27

26

25

439

SW Boulder Rd.

Joshua P. Free 11-14-36

Samuel K. McGee 10-12-32

Samuel K. McGee 7-5-37

Joshua P. Free 11-14-36

Jeremiah McDonald 9-14-36

Samuel K. McGee 7-5-37

442

Jacob Crandall 5-12-37

Samuel K. McGee 9-14-36

Jeremiah McDonald 4-11-32

Samuel K. McGee 9-14-36

John Reynolds 12-4-37

Jacob Crandall 5-12-37

Samuel K. McGee 9-14-36

Jeremiah McDonald 4-11-32

Samuel K. McGee 9-14-36

John Reynolds 12-4-37

Randolph McDonald 8-2-39

34

35

36

440

Samuel K. McGee 2-14-37

Samuel K. McGee 12-1-37

Jeremiah McDonald 1-5-36

Samuel K. McGee 2-14-37

Samuel K. McGee 12-1-37

Jeremiah McDonald 1-5-36

W Price Dr.

RAY COUNTY (area added to Ray in 1839)

TOWNSHIP 10

[Rockford, SE]

N
W   E
S

Miles

0   0.5   1.0

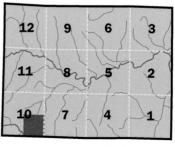

12	9	6	3
11	8	5	2
10	7	4	1

Area enlarged above

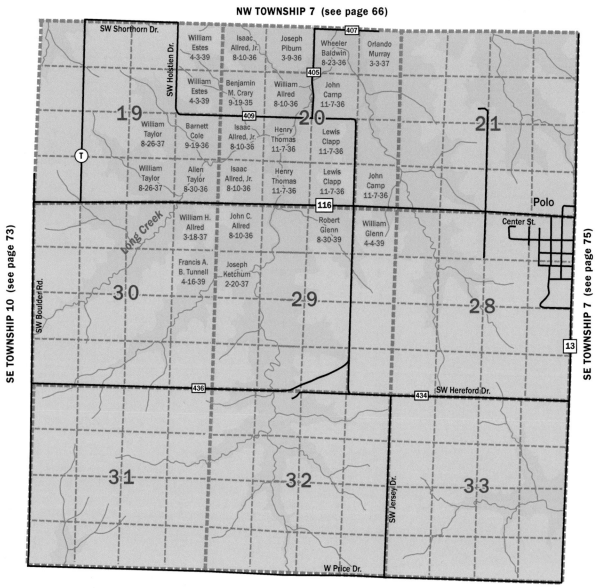

NW TOWNSHIP 7 (see page 66)

SW Shorthorn Dr.

SW Holstien Dr.

407

William Estes 4-3-39

Isaac Allred, Jr. 8-10-36

Joseph Piburn 3-9-36

Wheeler Baldwin 8-23-36

Orlando Murray 3-3-37

405

William Estes 4-3-39

Benjamin M. Crary 9-19-35

William Allred 8-10-36

John Camp 11-7-36

19

409

William Taylor 8-26-37

Barnett Cole 9-19-36

Isaac Allred, Jr. 8-10-36

Henry Thomas 11-7-36

20

Lewis Clapp 11-7-36

21

T

William Taylor 8-26-37

Allen Taylor 8-30-36

Isaac Allred, Jr. 8-10-36

Henry Thomas 11-7-36

Lewis Clapp 11-7-36

John Camp 11-7-36

116

Polo

Center St.

SE TOWNSHIP 10 (see page 73)

Long Creek

SW Boulder Rd.

William H. Allred 3-18-37

John C. Allred 8-10-36

Robert Glenn 8-30-39

William Glenn 4-4-39

SE TOWNSHIP 7 (see page 75)

Francis A. B. Tunnell 4-16-39

Joseph Ketchum 2-20-37

30

29

28

13

436

SW Hereford Dr.

434

31

32

SW Jersey Dr.

33

W Price Dr.

RAY COUNTY (area added to Ray in 1839)

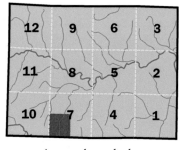

12   9   6   3

11   8   5   2

10   7   4   1

Area enlarged above

TOWNSHIP 7

[Grant, SW]

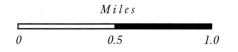

Miles

0   0.5   1.0

N

W   E

S

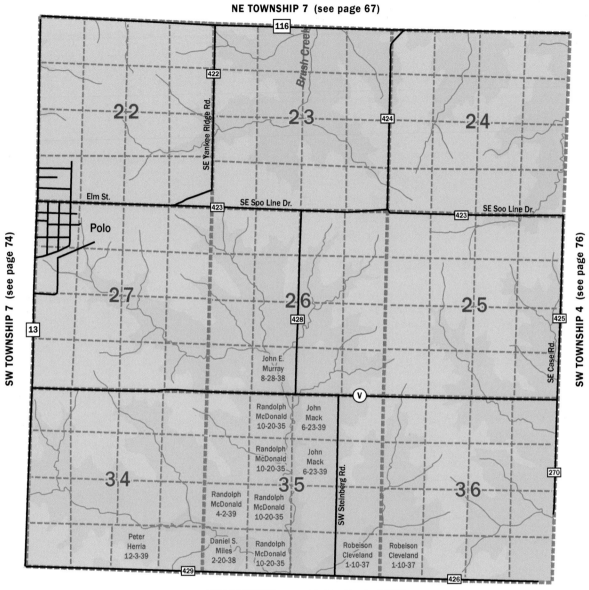

NE TOWNSHIP 7 (see page 67)

SW TOWNSHIP 7 (see page 74)

SW TOWNSHIP 4 (see page 76)

Brush Creek

SE Yankee Ridge Rd.

Elm St.

Polo

SE Soo Line Dr.

SE Soo Line Dr.

SE Case Rd.

SW Steinberg Rd.

22

23

24

27

26

25

34

35

36

John E. Murray
8-28-38

Randolph McDonald
10-20-35

John Mack
6-23-39

Randolph McDonald
10-20-35

John Mack
6-23-39

Randolph McDonald
4-2-39

Randolph McDonald
10-20-35

Peter Herria
12-3-39

Daniel S. Miles
2-20-38

Randolph McDonald
10-20-35

Robeison Cleveland
1-10-37

Robeison Cleveland
1-10-37

RAY COUNTY (area added to Ray in 1839)

TOWNSHIP 7

[Grant, SE]

N
W   E
S

Miles

0   0.5   1.0

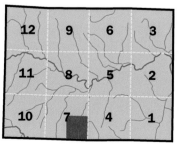

12	9	6	3
11	8	5	2
10	7	4	1

Area enlarged above

NW TOWNSHIP 4 (see page 68)

Crabapple Creek

19

20

21

Cowgill

SE Wildlife Rd.

SE Soo Line Dr.

SE TOWNSHIP 7 (see page 75)

SE Rock Island Rd.

SE Case Rd.

SE Apache Rd.

SE Frog Pond Rd.

SE Red Brick Rd.

30

29

28

Allen H. Thompson 7-17-38

Allen H. Thompson 7-17-38

SE Cottage Grove Dr.

SE TOWNSHIP 4 (see page 77)

Ⓑ

Ⓥ

James Frazier 10-1-34

James Frazier 10-1-34

Allen Thompson 1-27-36

Allen H. Thompson 1-29-38

James Lee 8-19-34

SE International Rd.

31

32

33

E Price Dr.

RAY COUNTY (area added to Ray in 1839)

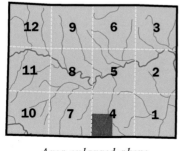

12	9	6	3
11	8	5	2
10	7	4	1

Area enlarged above

TOWNSHIP 4

[Lincoln, SW]

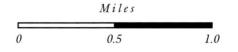

Miles

0　　　　　0.5　　　　　1.0

N

W   E

S

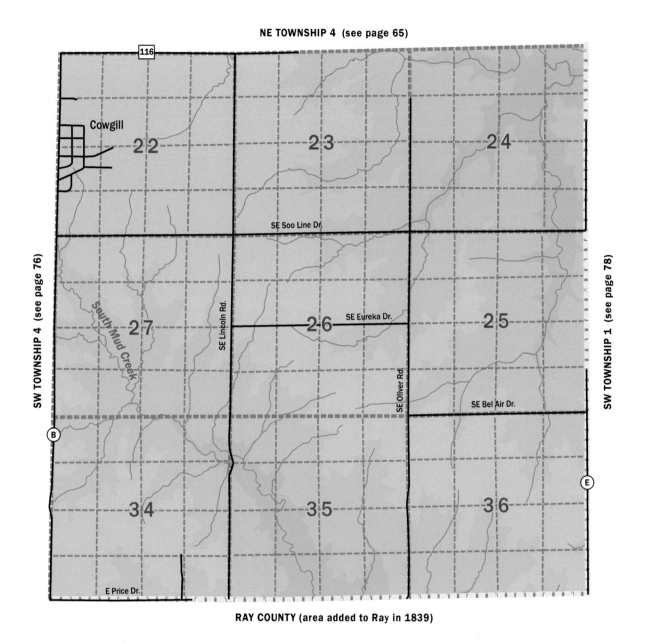

NE TOWNSHIP 4 (see page 65)

Cowgill

22 23 24

SE Soo Line Dr.

SW TOWNSHIP 4 (see page 76)

SW TOWNSHIP 1 (see page 78)

South Mud Creek

27 SE Lincoln Rd. 26 SE Eureka Dr. 25

SE Oliver Rd.

SE Bel Air Dr.

34 35 36

E Price Dr.

RAY COUNTY (area added to Ray in 1839)

TOWNSHIP 4

[Lincoln, SE]

N
W   E
S

Miles

0   0.5   1.0

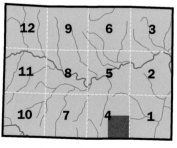

12	9	6	3
11	8	5	2
10	7	4	1

Area enlarged above

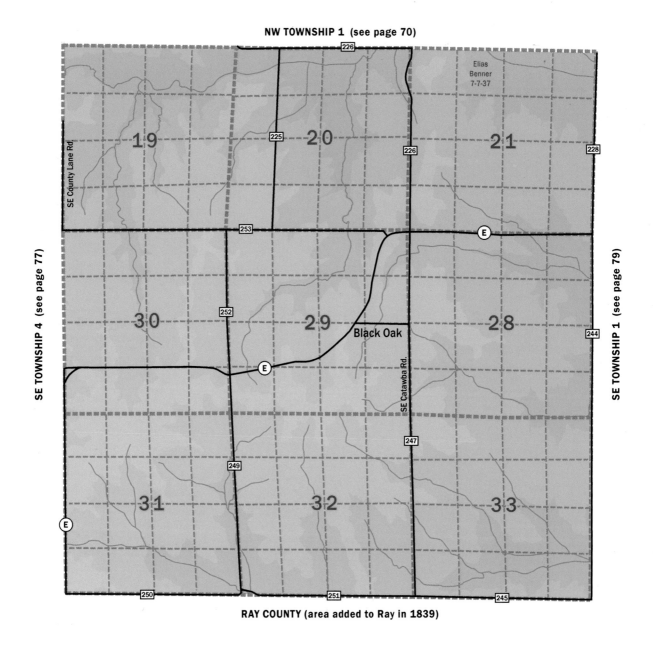

NW TOWNSHIP 1 (see page 70)

SE TOWNSHIP 4 (see page 77)

SE TOWNSHIP 1 (see page 79)

SE County Lane Rd.

Elias Benner 7-7-37

19

20

21

30

29

28

Black Oak

SE Catawba Rd.

31

32

33

RAY COUNTY (area added to Ray in 1839)

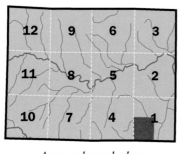

Area enlarged above

TOWNSHIP 1

[Davis, SW]

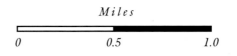

Miles

0   0.5   1.0

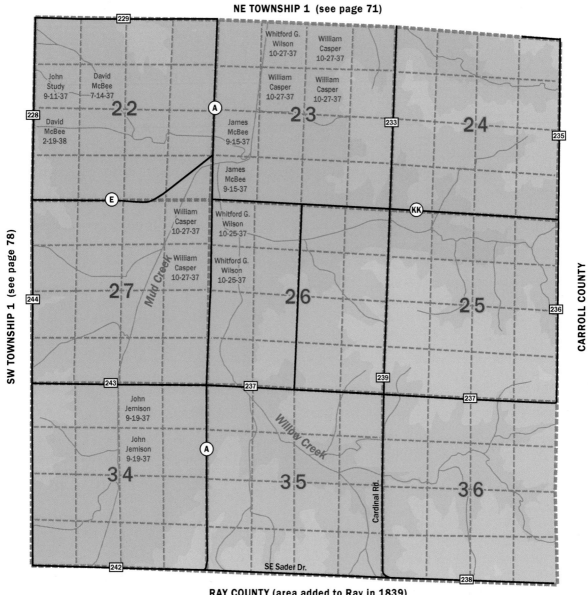

NE TOWNSHIP 1 (see page 71)

229

Whitford G.
Wilson
10-27-37

William
Casper
10-27-37

John
Study
9-11-37

David
McBee
7-14-37

William
Casper
10-27-37

William
Casper
10-27-37

228

David
McBee
2-19-38

22

A

James
McBee
9-15-37

23

233

24

235

James
McBee
9-15-37

E

KK

SW TOWNSHIP 1 (see page 78)

William
Casper
10-27-37

Whitford G.
Wilson
10-25-37

244

William
Casper
10-27-37

Whitford G.
Wilson
10-25-37

Mud Creek

27

26

25

236

243

237

239

237

John
Jemison
9-19-37

John
Jemison
9-19-37

A

Willow Creek

34

35

Cardinal Rd.

36

242

SE Sader Dr.

238

RAY COUNTY (area added to Ray in 1839)

CARROLL COUNTY

TOWNSHIP 1

[Davis, SE]

N
W   E
S

Miles

0   0.5   1.0

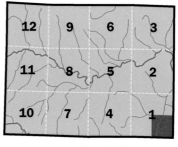

12	9	6	3
11	8	5	2
10	7	4	1

Area enlarged above

Index of Landowners

T HE FOLLOWING INDEX lists all the land purchasers in Caldwell County through 1839 as recorded in *An Index to Early Caldwell County, Missouri Land Records.* Purchasers are listed in alphabetical order by last name. Under the purchaser's name, there is a line for each quarter quarter section of land purchased.[1] For each parcel, the index lists the numbered statute township (Twp 1 – Twp 12), the numbered section within that township (1–36), the quarter quarter section by direction (NE, NW, SW, SE) within each quarter section (NE, NW, SW, SE) and finally the page number where the parcel is mapped in this atlas.

> EXAMPLE:
>
> **Abbott, Rufus**
>
> Twp 10 Sec 12 SE ¼ of NE ¼............65

In this example, Rufus Abbott owns a single quarter quarter section. It is located in section 12 of statute township 10 — i.e., section 12 of present-day Rockford Township. Rufus' land is the southeastern quarter quarter section (SE ¼) of the northeastern quarter (NE ¼) of the section. When you turn to page 35 in the atlas, you will see Rufus' 40 acres of land. Under Rufus' name on the map itself is the date of purchase, in this case "5-19-37," or May 19, 1837.

For an illustration of how townships are divided into sections and further subdivided into quarter quarter sections, see Map 9 on page 13.

---

[1] In *An Index to Early Caldwell County, Missouri Land Records*, when land was purchased in a larger quantity (e.g., a half quarter section or a full quarter section), the full purchase receives only one entry. I have divided all these purchases into the quarter quarter section components to show the entire grid on the atlas. As a result, larger parcels of land with single entries in the land records index have multiple entries in the index which follows in this atlas.

Abbott, Hiram
Twp 10 Sec 1 NE ¼ of NE ¼........ 65
Twp 10 Sec 1 SW ¼ of NE ¼........ 65

Abbott, Rufus
Twp 10 Sec 12 SE ¼ of NE ¼........ 65

Aldrich, Jamon
Twp 10 Sec 13 NE ¼ of NE ¼...... 65

Aldridge, James H.
Twp 11 Sec 33 NW ¼ of SE ¼...... 56

Alexander, Horace
Twp 2 Sec 11 SW ¼ of NE ¼..... 55
Twp 2 Sec 11 SE ¼ of NE ¼........ 55

Alexander, Randolph
Twp 11 Sec 21 SE ¼ of SE ¼........ 56
Twp 11 Sec 28 NW ¼ of NE ¼..... 56
Twp 11 Sec 28 SW ¼ of NE ¼...... 56

Allen, Alban
Twp 11 Sec 23 NW ¼ of SE ¼...... 57

Allen, Albern
Twp 8 Sec 32 NE ¼ of NW ¼....... 58
Twp 8 Sec 32 SE ¼ of NW ¼....... 58
Twp 8 Sec 32 NE ¼ of SW ¼....... 58
Twp 8 Sec 32 SW ¼ of SE ¼......... 58

Allen, James
Twp 11 Sec 28 NW ¼ of SE ¼...... 56
Twp 11 Sec 28 SW ¼ of SE ¼....... 56

Allred, Isaac Jr.
Twp 7 Sec 20 NW ¼ of NW ¼...... 74
Twp 7 Sec 20 NW ¼ of SW ¼...... 74
Twp 7 Sec 20 SW ¼ of SW ¼........ 74

Allred, James
Twp 7 Sec 6 NW ¼ of SW ¼......... 66
Twp 10 Sec 1 SE ¼ of NE ¼......... 65
Twp 10 Sec 1 NW ¼ of SE ¼....... 65

Allred, John C.
Twp 7 Sec 29 NW ¼ of NW ¼...... 74

Allred, Martin C.
Twp 10 Sec 2 NW ¼ of SE ¼........ 65
Twp 10 Sec 12 NW ¼ of SW ¼..... 65

Allred, Reuben W.
Twp 10 Sec 1 NE ¼ of SE ¼........ 65
Twp 10 Sec 1 SW ¼ of SE ¼......... 65

Allred, Wiley P.
Twp 10 Sec 13 NW ¼ of NE ¼..... 65

Allred, William
Twp 7 Sec 9 NW ¼ of SW ¼......... 66
Twp 7 Sec 17 NE ¼ of SW ¼........ 66
Twp 7 Sec 20 SE ¼ of NW ¼........ 74

Allred, William H.
Twp 7 Sec 18 NW ¼ of NW ¼...... 66

Twp 7 Sec 18 SW ¼ of NW ¼........ 66
Twp 7 Sec 18 NE ¼ of SW ¼........ 66
Twp 7 Sec 18 NW ¼ of SE ¼........ 66
Twp 7 Sec 30 NE ¼ of NE ¼........ 74
Twp 11 Sec 31 NW ¼ of NE ¼...... 56
Twp 11 Sec 31 SW ¼ of NE ¼...... 56

Alvord, Elisha
Twp 11 Sec 25 NE ¼ of NE ¼...... 57

Ames, Rial
Twp 10 Sec 28 SE ¼ of SE ¼........ 72

Anderson, John
Twp 8 Sec 7 SW ¼ of NW ¼......... 50
Twp 8 Sec 7 SE ¼ of NW ¼.......... 50
Twp 11 Sec 7 SE ¼ of NW ¼........ 48

Andrus, Milo
Twp 8 Sec 17 SE ¼ of NW ¼........ 50

Annis, James
Twp 12 Sec 4 SW ¼ of SW ¼........ 32
Twp 12 Sec 9 SW ¼ of NE ¼........ 32

Annis, John C.
Twp 10 Sec 4 SE ¼ of NW ¼........ 64
Twp 10 Sec 4 NE ¼ of SW ¼........ 64
Twp 12 Sec 9 NE ¼ of NW ¼........ 32
Twp 12 Sec 9 SE ¼ of NW ¼........ 32

Arbuckle, Samuel & Hudgins
Twp 2 Sec 34 NW ¼ of NW ¼...... 63
Twp 2 Sec 34 SW ¼ of NW ¼...... 63

Archer, John
Twp 12 Sec 17 SE ¼ of SW ¼....... 32

Ardinger, John H.
Twp 8 Sec 13 NE ¼ of SW ¼........ 51

Babbit, Loren
Twp 12 Sec 29 NE ¼ of SW ¼...... 40

Babcock, Dolphin
Twp 8 Sec 32 NW ¼ of SE ¼........ 58

Baldwin, Wheeler
Twp 7 Sec 20 NW ¼ of NE ¼....... 74

Ballard, Phillip
Twp 5 Sec 18 SW ¼ of SE ¼......... 52
Twp 5 Sec 18 SE ¼ of SE ¼.......... 52

Barnard, John P.
Twp 8 Sec 25 SW ¼ of SW ¼........ 59

Barton, Asa
Twp 12 Sec 29 NW ¼ of SE ¼...... 40
Twp 12 Sec 29 NE ¼ of SE ¼....... 40
Twp 12 Sec 29 SW ¼ of SE ¼....... 40

Barton, John
Twp 12 Sec 29 NW ¼ of NE ¼..... 40
Twp 12 Sec 29 SW ¼ of NE ¼...... 40

Batson, William
Twp 10 Sec 5 SW ¼ of SW ¼........ 64
Twp 10 Sec 6 SE ¼ of SE ¼.......... 64

Batterick, Aaron
Twp 10 Sec 11 NE ¼ of SE ¼....... 65

Bebe, George
Twp 11 Sec 22 NE ¼ of SE ¼....... 57
Twp 11 Sec 22 SE ¼ of SE ¼........ 57

Bedford, John
Twp 11 Sec 36 NE ¼ of SW ¼...... 57

Beebe, Calvin
Twp 8 Sec 7 SE ¼ of SE ¼........... 50
Twp 8 Sec 18 NE ¼ of NE ¼........ 50
Twp 8 Sec 18 SE ¼ of NW ¼........ 50
Twp 8 Sec 18 SE ¼ of NE ¼......... 50
Twp 11 Sec 13 SE ¼ of SE ¼........ 49
Twp 11 Sec 23 SE ¼ of SW ¼....... 57
Twp 11 Sec 26 SE ¼ of NW ¼...... 57

Beebe, George
Twp 11 Sec 23 NE ¼ of SW ¼...... 57

Beebe, Isaac
Twp 11 Sec 4 NW ¼ of NE ¼....... 48
Twp 11 Sec 4 NE ¼ of NE ¼........ 48
Twp 11 Sec 27 NE ¼ of NE ¼...... 57

Beech, Julius
Twp 11 Sec 25 NW ¼ of NW ¼.... 57
Twp 11 Sec 25 SW ¼ of NW ¼..... 57

Beecher, Ransom A.
Twp 8 Sec 2 NW ¼ of NE ¼......... 51
Twp 8 Sec 2 SW ¼ of NE ¼.......... 51
Twp 9 Sec 35 SE ¼ of SW ¼......... 43

Benjamin, Naham
Twp 8 Sec 26 SE ¼ of SE ¼.......... 59

Benjamin, Timothy N.
Twp 8 Sec 27 NE ¼ of SE ¼......... 59

Benner, Elias
Twp 1 Sec 21 NE ¼ of NW ¼....... 78

Benson, Alvah
Twp 11 Sec 3 SW ¼ of SE ¼......... 49

Benson, Benjamin
Twp 11 Sec 2 NW ¼ of SE ¼........ 49
Twp 11 Sec 2 SW ¼ of SE ¼......... 49

Benson, Jerome M.
Twp 10 Sec 14 NE ¼ of NE ¼...... 65
Twp 11 Sec 23 SW ¼ of NE ¼...... 57
Twp 11 Sec 23 NE ¼ of SE ¼....... 57

Bentley, Johnson
Twp 5 Sec 20 NE ¼ of SW ¼........ 60

Billings, Samuel
Twp 11 Sec 12 NE ¼ of SE ¼....... 49

Twp 12 Sec 24 NW ¼ of NE ¼..... 41

Billings, Titus
Twp 11 Sec 12 NE ¼ of SW ¼...... 49
Twp 12 Sec 24 NE ¼ of NE ¼...... 41
Twp 12 Sec 24 SE ¼ of NE ¼....... 41
Twp 12 Sec 28 NE ¼ of NW ¼..... 40
Twp 12 Sec 28 SE ¼ of NW ¼...... 40

Billington, Ezekiel
Twp 11 Sec 29 SE ¼ of NW ¼...... 56
Twp 11 Sec 30 NE ¼ of SW ¼...... 56
Twp 11 Sec 30 SE ¼ of SW ¼...... 56

Blackburn, Anthony
Twp 2 Sec 3 SE ¼ of NE ¼........... 55
Twp 2 Sec 3 NE ¼ of SE ¼........... 55

Bolds, Thomas
Twp 5 Sec 11 SE ¼ of SE ¼.......... 53

Borst, William M.
Twp 7 Sec 7 SW ¼ of NE ¼.......... 66
Twp 7 Sec 7 NW ¼ of SE ¼.......... 66
Twp 7 Sec 7 SW ¼ of SE ¼.......... 66
Twp 7 Sec 18 NE ¼ of NE ¼........ 66

Bozorth, Abner
Twp 10 Sec 11 SW ¼ of NE ¼...... 65
Twp 11 Sec 4 NE ¼ of NW ¼....... 48
Twp 11 Sec 17 NE ¼ of SE ¼....... 48
Twp 11 Sec 17 SE ¼ of SE ¼....... 48
Twp 11 Sec 18 NW ¼ of SW ¼..... 48
Twp 11 Sec 18 SW ¼ of SW ¼..... 48
Twp 11 Sec 19 NE ¼ of SE ¼....... 56
Twp 11 Sec 31 NE ¼ of NE ¼....... 56
Twp 11 Sec 31 NW ¼ of SW ¼..... 56

Bozorth, John
Twp 8 Sec 31 SW ¼ of NE ¼........ 58
Twp 11 Sec 15 NW ¼ of SW ¼...... 49
Twp 11 Sec 15 SW ¼ of SW ¼...... 49
Twp 11 Sec 29 NE ¼ of SE ¼....... 56
Twp 11 Sec 29 SE ¼ of SE ¼....... 56
Twp 11 Sec 33 NW ¼ of NW ¼..... 56
Twp 11 Sec 33 NE ¼ of NW ¼..... 56
Twp 11 Sec 33 SW ¼ of NW ¼..... 56
Twp 11 Sec 34 SW ¼ of NE ¼...... 57
Twp 11 Sec 34 NW ¼ of SE ¼...... 57

Bozorth, Squire
Twp 11 Sec 9 NE ¼ of SW ¼........ 48
Twp 11 Sec 9 SE ¼ of SW ¼........ 48
Twp 11 Sec 11 NW ¼ of NE ¼...... 49
Twp 11 Sec 11 SW ¼ of NE ¼...... 49
Twp 11 Sec 15 NW ¼ of NW ¼..... 49
Twp 11 Sec 15 SW ¼ of NW ¼..... 49
Twp 11 Sec 20 NE ¼ of NE ¼....... 56
Twp 11 Sec 20 NE ¼ of SW ¼...... 56
Twp 11 Sec 20 SE ¼ of SW ¼....... 56
Twp 11 Sec 21 NW ¼ of NW ¼..... 56
Twp 11 Sec 21 SW ¼ of NW ¼..... 56
Twp 11 Sec 29 NE ¼ of NE ¼....... 56
Twp 11 Sec 29 NW ¼ of SE ¼...... 56

Twp 11 Sec 29 SW ¼ of SE ¼...... 56
Twp 11 Sec 33 NW ¼ of NE ¼..... 56
Twp 11 Sec 33 SW ¼ of NE ¼..... 56
Twp 11 Sec 33 NW ¼ of SW ¼..... 56
Twp 11 Sec 33 NE ¼ of SW ¼...... 56
Twp 11 Sec 33 SW ¼ of SW ¼...... 56

Brace, Truman
Twp 9 Sec 17 NW ¼ of NW ¼..... 34

Bracken, Levi
Twp 7 Sec 7 SW ¼ of SW ¼.......... 66

Bradley, Abijah
Twp 6 Sec 32 NE ¼ of SE ¼........ 44

Bradley, Alijah
Twp 8 Sec 11 NE ¼ of SE ¼........ 51

Brady, Lindsey A.
Twp 2 Sec 7 NW ¼ of SE ¼.......... 54
Twp 10 Sec 10 NE ¼ of SW ¼...... 65

Brady, Linsey A.
Twp 2 Sec 6 NW ¼ of SE ¼.......... 54

Bragg, Benjamin
Twp 10 Sec 11 SE ¼ of SW ¼....... 65

Brown, Alanson
Twp 11 Sec 8 NE ¼ of NW ¼..... 48
Twp 11 Sec 12 NW ¼ of NE ¼..... 49

Brown, Ebenezer
Twp 8 Sec 30 NE ¼ of NE ¼........ 58

Brown, Guersey
Twp 8 Sec 30 NW ¼ of NE ¼...... 58
Twp 8 Sec 30 SW ¼ of NE ¼....... 58

Brown, Sherman
Twp 8 Sec 36 NE ¼ of NW ¼...... 59

Burk, John M.
Twp 8 Sec 7 SW ¼ of SW ¼.......... 50

Burke, John M.
Twp 11 Sec 21 SE ¼ of NE ¼....... 56

Burnett, Peter H.
Twp 11 Sec 4 SW ¼ of NW ¼....... 48
Twp 11 Sec 4 SE ¼ of NW ¼....... 48
Twp 11 Sec 4 NE ¼ of SE ¼....... 48
Twp 11 Sec 4 SE ¼ of SE ¼....... 48
Twp 12 Sec 28 NE ¼ of SE ¼...... 40
Twp 12 Sec 28 SE ¼ of SE ¼...... 40

Burnham, James
Twp 8 Sec 33 NE ¼ of SE ¼......... 58

Burton, John N.
Twp 8 Sec 28 NE ¼ of SW ¼......... 58

Butler, Armond
Twp 11 Sec 9 SE ¼ of NW ¼........ 48

Butler, John L.
Twp 11 Sec 26 NE ¼ of SW ¼..... 57

Twp 11 Sec 26 NW ¼ of SE ¼..... 57
Twp 11 Sec 26 SE ¼ of SW ¼....... 57

Butts, William L.
Twp 10 Sec 1 NW ¼ of NW ¼...... 65

Cady, Arthur
Twp 5 Sec 15 NW ¼ of NW ¼...... 53

Caffey, Henry
Twp 10 Sec 30 SW ¼ of SW ¼...... 72
Twp 10 Sec 31 NW ¼ of NW ¼.... 72

Camp, John
Twp 7 Sec 20 SW ¼ of NE ¼........ 74
Twp 7 Sec 20 SE ¼ of SE ¼.......... 74

Campbell, William
Twp 12 Sec 26 SE ¼ of SW ¼....... 41

Carill, John
Twp 11 Sec 3 NE ¼ of NW ¼...... 49
Twp 11 Sec 3 SE ¼ of NW ¼........ 49

Carrell, Nancy
Twp 8 Sec 18 SW ¼ of NW ¼....... 50

Carroll, James
Twp 10 Sec 6 NW ¼ of SW ¼...... 64

Carroll, Jesse M.
Twp 10 Sec 11 SW ¼ of SE ¼....... 65

Carson, George
Twp 12 Sec 18 NW ¼ of NE ¼..... 32

Carson, William H.
Twp 12 Sec 18 SW ¼ of NE ¼..... 32

Carter, Orlando H.
Twp 11 Sec 32 NE ¼ of SW ¼...... 56

Carter, Simeon
Twp 10 Sec 6 NE ¼ of NE ¼........ 64
Twp 11 Sec 31 NE ¼ of SE ¼....... 56
Twp 11 Sec 31 SE ¼ of SE ¼........ 56
Twp 11 Sec 32 SE ¼ of SW ¼....... 56

Casper, William
Twp 1 Sec 23 NW ¼ of NE ¼...... 79
Twp 1 Sec 23 SE ¼ of NW ¼...... 79
Twp 1 Sec 23 SW ¼ of NE ¼...... 79
Twp 1 Sec 27 NE ¼ of NE ¼...... 79
Twp 1 Sec 27 SE ¼ of NE ¼...... 79
Twp 3 Sec 11 NE ¼ of NW ¼...... 39
Twp 3 Sec 11 SE ¼ of NW ¼........ 39

Clapp, Lewis
Twp 7 Sec 20 NW ¼ of SE ¼...... 74
Twp 7 Sec 20 SW ¼ of SE ¼......... 74

Clark, Isaac
Twp 5 Sec 12 SW ¼ of SW ¼........ 53

Clark, James C.
Twp 10 Sec 19 NE ¼ of SW ¼...... 72
Twp 10 Sec 19 NW ¼ of SE ¼...... 72

Twp 10 Sec 19 SE ¼ of SW ¼........ 72
Twp 10 Sec 19 SW ¼ of SE ¼........ 72
Twp 10 Sec 31 SW ¼ of NW ¼..... 72

Clark, John W.

Twp 11 Sec 32 NE ¼ of SE ¼ 56

Clark, Joseph

Twp 11 Sec 5 SW ¼ of NE ¼........ 48
Twp 11 Sec 5 SE ¼ of NE ¼......... 48
Twp 12 Sec 14 NE ¼ of NE ¼...... 33
Twp 12 Sec 14 SE ¼ of NE ¼....... 33
Twp 12 Sec 14 NW ¼ of SE ¼...... 33
Twp 12 Sec 14 NE ¼ of SE ¼....... 33

Clark, Timothy B.

Twp 10 Sec 2 NW ¼ of NW ¼...... 65
Twp 10 Sec 2 NE ¼ of NW ¼........ 65
Twp 10 Sec 2 SW ¼ of NW ¼....... 65
Twp 10 Sec 2 SE ¼ of NW ¼........ 65
Twp 10 Sec 10 NE ¼ of SE ¼........ 65
Twp 10 Sec 10 SE ¼ of SE ¼......... 65
Twp 11 Sec 23 SE ¼ of NE ¼....... 57

Clark, William C.

Twp 10 Sec 11 SE ¼ of NE ¼....... 65

Clark, William O.

Twp 7 Sec 18 NE ¼ of NW ¼....... 66
Twp 7 Sec 18 SE ¼ of NW ¼....... 66

Clauson, Moses

Twp 8 Sec 30 NE ¼ of SE ¼......... 58
Twp 8 Sec 31 NE ¼ of NE ¼........ 58
Twp 8 Sec 31 SE ¼ of NE ¼......... 58

Cleavinger, Jesse Jr.

Twp 11 Sec 23 NW ¼ of SW ¼..... 57
Twp 11 Sec 23 SW ¼ of SW ¼...... 57

Clemmson, John

Twp 11 Sec 12 NW ¼ of SE ¼...... 49
Twp 11 Sec 12 SW ¼ of SE ¼....... 49

Cleveland, Robeison

Twp 7 Sec 35 SE ¼ of SE ¼.......... 75
Twp 7 Sec 36 SW ¼ of SW ¼....... 75

Clothier, Ira

Twp 11 Sec 9 NW ¼ of NE ¼....... 48
Twp 11 Sec 9 SW ¼ of NE ¼........ 48
Twp 11 Sec 11 SW ¼ of NW ¼..... 49

Cole, Barnett

Twp 7 Sec 19 NE ¼ of SE ¼....... 74

Cole, Zarah S.

Twp 11 Sec 13 SE ¼ of NW ¼....... 49

Colvin, Samuel

Twp 3 Sec 1 SE ¼ of NW ¼.......... 39
Twp 3 Sec 1 SW ¼ of SW ¼.......... 39
Twp 3 Sec 1 SE ¼ of SW ¼........... 39
Twp 3 Sec 11 NW ¼ of SW ¼....... 39
Twp 3 Sec 11 SW ¼ of SW ¼........ 39

Conner, John

Twp 3 Sec 2 NW ¼ of NW ¼........ 39
Twp 3 Sec 2 NE ¼ of NW ¼......... 39
Twp 3 Sec 2 SW ¼ of NW ¼......... 39
Twp 3 Sec 2 SE ¼ of NW ¼.......... 39
Twp 3 Sec 2 NE ¼ of SW ¼.......... 39
Twp 3 Sec 11 NW ¼ of NW ¼....... 39
Twp 3 Sec 11 SW ¼ of NW ¼....... 39
Twp 3 Sec 11 SW ¼ of NE ¼........ 39

Conner, Livingston

Twp 3 Sec 11 NW ¼ of NE ¼....... 39

Cooper, John

Twp 10 Sec 15 NW ¼ of NE ¼..... 65
Twp 10 Sec 15 SE ¼ of NW ¼...... 65

Coots, Abraham

Twp 8 Sec 22 NW ¼ of SW ¼....... 59
Twp 8 Sec 22 SW ¼ of SW ¼........ 59
Twp 8 Sec 27 NE ¼ of SW ¼........ 59
Twp 8 Sec 27 SE ¼ of SW ¼......... 59
Twp 8 Sec 28 NE ¼ of SE ¼......... 58
Twp 8 Sec 28 SW ¼ of SE ¼......... 58

Corey, Benjamin

Twp 11 Sec 21 SE ¼ of NW ¼...... 56

Corrill, John

Twp 11 Sec 2 NW ¼ of NE ¼....... 49
Twp 11 Sec 2 SW ¼ of NE ¼........ 49

Cowdery, Oliver

Twp 8 Sec 30 NW ¼ of SE ¼........ 58
Twp 8 Sec 30 SW ¼ of SE ¼......... 58
Twp 8 Sec 31 NW ¼ of NW ¼....... 58
Twp 8 Sec 31 NE ¼ of NW ¼........ 58
Twp 8 Sec 31 SW ¼ of NW ¼........ 58
Twp 8 Sec 31 SE ¼ of NW ¼......... 58
Twp 11 Sec 25 NW ¼ of SW ¼..... 57
Twp 11 Sec 25 NE ¼ of SW ¼....... 57
Twp 11 Sec 25 SW ¼ of SW ¼....... 57
Twp 11 Sec 25 SE ¼ of SW ¼........ 57
Twp 11 Sec 36 NE ¼ of NE ¼....... 57
Twp 11 Sec 36 SE ¼ of NE ¼........ 57
Twp 12 Sec 26 NW ¼ of SE ¼...... 41
Twp 12 Sec 26 SW ¼ of SE ¼....... 41
Twp 12 Sec 35 NW ¼ of NE ¼...... 41
Twp 12 Sec 35 SW ¼ of NE ¼...... 41

Cowen, Horace

Twp 11 Sec 12 SE ¼ of SW ¼....... 49

Cox, Frederick W.

Twp 10 Sec 5 NE ¼ of SW ¼........ 64
Twp 10 Sec 5 NW ¼ of SE ¼........ 64
Twp 10 Sec 29 SE ¼ of NE ¼....... 72

Cox, Solomon

Twp 8 Sec 25 NE ¼ of NE ¼........ 59
Twp 8 Sec 25 SE ¼ of NE ¼......... 59

Crandal, Jacob

Twp 10 Sec 27 NW ¼ of NW ¼.... 73

Crandall, Jacob

Twp 10 Sec 34 NW ¼ of NW ¼.... 73
Twp 10 Sec 34 SW ¼ of NW ¼..... 73

Crandall, John W.

Twp 10 Sec 28 NE ¼ of NE ¼...... 72

Crandall, Thomas

Twp 10 Sec 30 NE ¼ of NW ¼..... 72
Twp 10 Sec 30 SW ¼ of NE ¼...... 72

Crary, Benjamin M.

Twp 7 Sec 20 SW ¼ of NW ¼....... 74

Creson, William

Twp 11 Sec 30 NW ¼ of SW ¼..... 56

Crowley, Hiram

Twp 10 Sec 32 NE ¼ of SW ¼...... 72

Crowley, James

Twp 7 Sec 18 SW ¼ of SW ¼........ 66
Twp 10 Sec 32 SE ¼ of NE ¼....... 72
Twp 10 Sec 32 NE ¼ of SE ¼....... 72

Crowley, Jeremiah

Twp 7 Sec 18 NW ¼ of SW ¼........ 66

Crowley, John

Twp 10 Sec 14 SW ¼ of SE ¼....... 65
Twp 10 Sec 31 NE ¼ of NE ¼...... 72
Twp 10 Sec 31 SE ¼ of NE ¼....... 72
Twp 10 Sec 31 NE ¼ of SE ¼....... 72
Twp 10 Sec 31 SE ¼ of SE ¼........ 72
Twp 10 Sec 32 NW ¼ of NE ¼..... 72
Twp 10 Sec 32 NW ¼ of SW ¼..... 72
Twp 10 Sec 32 SW ¼ of SW ¼...... 72
Twp 10 Sec 32 SE ¼ of SE ¼........ 72

Crowley, John Jr.

Twp 10 Sec 32 SW ¼ of NW ¼..... 72
Twp 10 Sec 32 SE ¼ of NW ¼...... 72

Culbertson, Robert

Twp 5 Sec 15 SW ¼ of SW ¼........ 53
Twp 5 Sec 22 NW ¼ of NW ¼...... 61
Twp 5 Sec 22 SW ¼ of NW ¼...... 61
Twp 5 Sec 27 NW ¼ of NW ¼...... 61
Twp 5 Sec 27 NW ¼ of NE ¼....... 61
Twp 5 Sec 27 SW ¼ of NE ¼........ 61
Twp 5 Sec 27 NW ¼ of SW ¼....... 61
Twp 5 Sec 27 NE ¼ of SW ¼........ 61
Twp 5 Sec 27 SW ¼ of SW ¼........ 61

Cunningham, Christopher

Twp 10 Sec 10 SE ¼ of NE ¼....... 65
Twp 10 Sec 10 NW ¼ of SE ¼...... 65
Twp 10 Sec 10 SW ¼ of SE ¼....... 65

Curtis, Charles P.

Twp 10 Sec 1 NE ¼ of SW ¼........ 65
Twp 10 Sec 1 SE ¼ of SW ¼......... 65

Curtis, Jeremiah

Twp 10 Sec 1 SE ¼ of SE ¼.......... 65

Twp 11 Sec 31 SW ¼ of NW ¼..... 56

Fisher, John B.

Twp 7 Sec 17 NW ¼ of SW ¼....... 66

Fletcher, Jesse

Twp 8 Sec 25 NW ¼ of SW ¼....... 59
Twp 8 Sec 25 NE ¼ of SW ¼....... 59
Twp 8 Sec 25 NW ¼ of SE ¼....... 59
Twp 8 Sec 25 SE ¼ of SW ¼....... 59
Twp 8 Sec 25 SW ¼ of SE ¼....... 59
Twp 8 Sec 26 NE ¼ of SE ¼....... 59

Fletcher, John

Twp 7 Sec 4 NE ¼ of NW ¼......... 66

Follett, King

Twp 11 Sec 9 NE ¼ of NW ¼...... 48

Foot, Reuben

Twp 7 Sec 5 NW ¼ of NW ¼........ 66
Twp 7 Sec 6 NE ¼ of NE ¼......... 66
Twp 7 Sec 6 SE ¼ of NE ¼........... 66

Foot, Timothy B.

Twp 7 Sec 5 NE ¼ of NW ¼......... 66
Twp 7 Sec 5 NW ¼ of NE ¼......... 66
Twp 7 Sec 5 SW ¼ of NW ¼......... 66
Twp 8 Sec 32 NW ¼ of SW ¼....... 58
Twp 8 Sec 32 SE ¼ of SW ¼........ 58

Foutz, Jacob

Twp 2 Sec 3 SW ¼ of NW ¼........ 55
Twp 2 Sec 3 NE ¼ of SW ¼......... 55
Twp 2 Sec 3 SE ¼ of SW ¼......... 55
Twp 2 Sec 9 SW ¼ of NE ¼......... 54
Twp 2 Sec 10 NW ¼ of SW ¼....... 55
Twp 2 Sec 10 SW ¼ of SW ¼....... 55

Frampton, David

Twp 12 Sec 29 SE ¼ of SW ¼....... 40

Frazier, James

Twp 4 Sec 32 NE ¼ of NW ¼....... 76
Twp 4 Sec 32 SE ¼ of NW ¼....... 76

Free, Joshua P.

Twp 10 Sec 27 NW ¼ of SW ¼..... 73
Twp 10 Sec 27 SW ¼ of SW ¼..... 73

Freeman, Nathan

Twp 3 Sec 12 NE ¼ of NE ¼........ 39

Freeman, Oliver

Twp 9 Sec 20 SE ¼ of NW ¼........ 42

French, Charles H.

Twp 8 Sec 27 NE ¼ of NW ¼....... 59
Twp 8 Sec 27 SW ¼ of NW ¼....... 59
Twp 8 Sec 27 SE ¼ of NW ¼....... 59

Frye, John

Twp 3 Sec 36 SW ¼ of SE ¼........ 47

Frye, William

Twp 9 Sec 31 NW ¼ of SW ¼....... 42

Twp 9 Sec 31 SW ¼ of SW ¼........ 42
Twp 11 Sec 25 NW ¼ of NE ¼..... 57
Twp 11 Sec 25 SW ¼ of NE ¼...... 57

Fryer, William

Twp 2 Sec 1 SE ¼ of NE ¼............ 55
Twp 3 Sec 36 NE ¼ of SW ¼........ 47

Fuller, Josiah

Twp 2 Sec 18 SW ¼ of SW ¼........ 54

Fuller, Lucius H.

Twp 10 Sec 14 SW ¼ of NE ¼...... 65
Twp 10 Sec 14 SE ¼ of NE ¼....... 65

Fuller, Samuel

Twp 7 Sec 7 SW ¼ of NW ¼......... 66

Gallaher, James

Twp 11 Sec 32 NW ¼ of NE ¼..... 56
Twp 11 Sec 32 SW ¼ of NE ¼...... 56

Gallaher, William Z.

Twp 11 Sec 32 NE ¼ of NE ¼...... 56

Gates, Jacob

Twp 11 Sec 20 SW ¼ of NE ¼...... 56
Twp 11 Sec 20 NW ¼ of SE ¼...... 56
Twp 11 Sec 21 NW ¼ of SW ¼..... 56

Gibbs, Luman

Twp 11 Sec 32 SE ¼ of SE ¼........ 56

Gilbert, William

Twp 5 Sec 9 SW ¼ of SE ¼........... 52

Givens, William

Twp 8 Sec 27 NW ¼ of SW ¼....... 59
Twp 8 Sec 27 NW ¼ of SE ¼........ 59

Glenn, Robert

Twp 7 Sec 29 NW ¼ of NE ¼....... 74

Glenn, William

Twp 7 Sec 29 NE ¼ of NE ¼........ 74

Grainger, Carlos

Twp 11 Sec 21 NE ¼ of SE ¼....... 56

Graves, Alvin C.

Twp 11 Sec 22 SW ¼ of SW ¼..... 57
Twp 11 Sec 22 SE ¼ of SW ¼...... 57

Graves, Thomas

Twp 7 Sec 8 SE ¼ of SE ¼............. 66

Graves, Warren

Twp 11 Sec 22 NE ¼ of SW ¼...... 57

Green, Francis H.

Twp 10 Sec 13 NE ¼ of SW ¼...... 65
Twp 10 Sec 13 SE ¼ of SW ¼....... 65
Twp 10 Sec 23 NE ¼ of NE ¼...... 73
Twp 10 Sec 24 NW ¼ of NW ¼.... 73
Twp 10 Sec 24 SW ¼ of NW ¼..... 73

Green, Harvey

Twp 10 Sec 3 NW ¼ of NW ¼...... 65

Twp 10 Sec 3 NE ¼ of NW ¼....... 65
Twp 10 Sec 4 NE ¼ of NE ¼........ 64

Gregg, John

Twp 5 Sec 21 NE ¼ of NE ¼........ 60
Twp 11 Sec 33 NE ¼ of SE ¼....... 56
Twp 11 Sec 34 SE ¼ of SW ¼...... 57
Twp 11 Sec 34 SW ¼ of SE ¼...... 57

Grover, Thomas

Twp 11 Sec 19 NW ¼ of SE ¼...... 56
Twp 11 Sec 20 NW ¼ of SW ¼..... 56
Twp 11 Sec 20 SW ¼ of SW ¼..... 56

Guffey, Ashley R.

Twp 2 Sec 7 NE ¼ of NW ¼......... 54

Guinn, David

Twp 11 Sec 34 SW ¼ of NW ¼..... 57
Twp 11 Sec 34 NW ¼ of SW ¼..... 57

Guinn, Henry

Twp 11 Sec 36 SW ¼ of NE ¼...... 57

Guinn, Thomas

Twp 8 Sec 30 NW ¼ of SW ¼....... 58
Twp 8 Sec 30 NE ¼ of SW ¼....... 58
Twp 8 Sec 30 SE ¼ of SW ¼........ 58

Guinn, Thorita

Twp 11 Sec 36 NW ¼ of NE ¼..... 57

Guyun, Daniel

Twp 11 Sec 25 NW ¼ of SE ¼...... 57
Twp 11 Sec 25 SW ¼ of SE ¼...... 57

Hamblin, Isaac

Twp 9 Sec 8 NE ¼ of SW ¼.......... 34
Twp 9 Sec 8 SE ¼ of SW ¼........... 34

Hammer, Austin

Twp 2 Sec 1 NW ¼ of NE ¼......... 55
Twp 2 Sec 1 NE ¼ of NE ¼.......... 55

Hancock, Alvah

Twp 10 Sec 28 NE ¼ of SE ¼....... 72

Hancock, Solomon

Twp 11 Sec 5 SE ¼ of SW ¼......... 48

Hancock, Thomas Sen.

Twp 11 Sec 29 NW ¼ of NW ¼.... 56
Twp 11 Sec 29 SW ¼ of NW ¼..... 56

Harding, Dwight

Twp 11 Sec 21 NE ¼ of SW ¼...... 56

Harlin, James

Twp 10 Sec 30 NE ¼ of SE ¼....... 72

Harper, William

Twp 8 Sec 13 NE ¼ of SE ¼......... 51

Harrier, Jacob

Twp 5 Sec 18 NE ¼ of SW ¼........ 52

Harris, George W.

Twp 11 Sec 3 SE ¼ of SE ¼.......... 49

Johnson, George
Twp 8 Sec 30 NW ¼ of NW ¼...... 58
Twp 8 Sec 30 SW ¼ of NW ¼...... 58
Twp 11 Sec 25 SE ¼ of NE ¼...... 57

Johnson, Jacob
Twp 10 Sec 5 NW ¼ of SW ¼...... 64

Johnson, James
Twp 8 Sec 30 SW ¼ of SW ¼........ 58

Johnson, Luke
Twp 11 Sec 8 SW ¼ of SE ¼......... 48

Johnson, Lyman E.
Twp 11 Sec 19 SE ¼ of SE ¼........ 56

Johnson, Mahlon
Twp 2 Sec 12 NE ¼ of SW ¼....... 55

Jones, Benjamin
Twp 10 Sec 10 SW ¼ of NE ¼...... 65
Twp 10 Sec 11 NE ¼ of SW ¼...... 65

Jones, David
Twp 12 Sec 31 SW ¼ of SW ¼...... 40

Jones, Granville
Twp 12 Sec 13 NW ¼ of NW ¼.... 33
Twp 12 Sec 13 SW ¼ of NW ¼..... 33

Jones, Spotswood
Twp 11 Sec 18 NW ¼ of SE ¼...... 48

Jones, William
Twp 10 Sec 5 NW ¼ of NW ¼...... 64
Twp 11 Sec 32 SW ¼ of SW ¼...... 56

Judy, David
Twp 11 Sec 1 SW ¼ of NE ¼........ 49

Kay, James
Twp 7 Sec 8 SW ¼ of SE ¼........... 66

Keeney, Abraham
Twp 5 Sec 21 NE ¼ of NW ¼....... 60
Twp 5 Sec 22 NW ¼ of SW ¼....... 61

Keeney, James
Twp 5 Sec 21 SE ¼ of NE ¼......... 60

Keeney, John
Twp 5 Sec 21 NE ¼ of SE ¼......... 60
Twp 5 Sec 21 SE ¼ of SE ¼.......... 60
Twp 5 Sec 22 SW ¼ of NW ¼....... 61

Kellsey, Samuel A.
Twp 12 Sec 34 NW ¼ of NW ¼.... 41

Kent, Horatio
Twp 7 Sec 4 NW ¼ of NE ¼......... 66
Twp 7 Sec 4 SW ¼ of NE ¼.......... 66

Kent, Horatio N.
Twp 7 Sec 4 SE ¼ of NW ¼.......... 66

Kenyon, Daniel
Twp 5 Sec 21 SE ¼ of SW ¼......... 60
Twp 8 Sec 13 NW ¼ of SE ¼....... 51
Twp 8 Sec 13 SW ¼ of SE ¼......... 51

Ketcham, Joseph
Twp 7 Sec 29 SW ¼ of NW ¼....... 74
Twp 10 Sec 24 NE ¼ of SW ¼...... 73

Keyes, Perry
Twp 10 Sec 7 NE ¼ of NE ¼........ 64

Killion, John
Twp 12 Sec 21 NW ¼ of NW ¼.... 40
Twp 12 Sec 21 SW ¼ of NW ¼.... 40
Twp 12 Sec 21 NW ¼ of SW ¼.... 40
Twp 12 Sec 21 SW ¼ of SW ¼...... 40

Kimbel, Samuel
Twp 11 Sec 26 SW ¼ of SE ¼....... 57

King, Thomas
Twp 11 Sec 29 NE ¼ of SW ¼...... 56
Twp 11 Sec 32 NW ¼ of NW ¼.... 56
Twp 11 Sec 32 NE ¼ of NW ¼.... 56
Twp 11 Sec 32 SW ¼ of NW ¼..... 56
Twp 11 Sec 32 SE ¼ of NW ¼...... 56

Kinyon, Daniel
Twp 5 Sec 18 NW ¼ of SW ¼....... 52
Twp 5 Sec 20 SE ¼ of SW ¼......... 60
Twp 8 Sec 15 NW ¼ of SE ¼........ 51

Knight, Joseph
Twp 8 Sec 18 NW ¼ of NW ¼...... 50

Knight, Newel
Twp 8 Sec 18 NW ¼ of SE ¼........ 50

Lain, John D.
Twp 5 Sec 19 NE ¼ of SW ¼........ 60
Twp 5 Sec 19 SE ¼ of SW ¼......... 60

Larkey, Edward
Twp 10 Sec 3 SE ¼ of SW ¼......... 65

Larkey, John
Twp 10 Sec 3 NE ¼ of SW ¼........ 65
Twp 10 Sec 3 NE ¼ of SE ¼......... 65
Twp 10 Sec 3 SE ¼ of SE ¼.......... 65
Twp 10 Sec 10 NW ¼ of NE ¼...... 65
Twp 10 Sec 10 NE ¼ of NE ¼...... 65
Twp 10 Sec 11 NW ¼ of NW ¼.... 65

Laskey, Edward
Twp 12 Sec 34 SW ¼ of SW ¼...... 41

Lee, Alfred
Twp 10 Sec 6 NW ¼ of NW ¼...... 64

Lee, Henry
Twp 8 Sec 15 SW ¼ of SE ¼......... 51

Lee, James
Twp 4 Sec 32 NE ¼ of SE ¼......... 76

Lee, Polly
Twp 5 Sec 12 SW ¼ of SE ¼......... 53

Leonard, Lyman
Twp 11 Sec 29 SW ¼ of SW ¼...... 56
Twp 11 Sec 29 SE ¼ of SW ¼...... 56

Lewis, David
Twp 2 Sec 17 NE ¼ of NE ¼........ 54
Twp 2 Sec 17 SE ¼ of NE ¼......... 54

Lillard, John C.
Twp 7 Sec 1 SE ¼ of NW ¼......... 67

Loveless, John
Twp 7 Sec 18 SE ¼ of SW ¼......... 66
Twp 10 Sec 13 SE ¼ of NE ¼...... 65

Lowell, Uriah B.
Twp 11 Sec 1 SW ¼ of NW ¼....... 49

Lowry, James
Twp 11 Sec 30 SE ¼ of NW ¼...... 56

Loy, Alfred
Twp 7 Sec 3 NW ¼ of NW ¼........ 67
Twp 7 Sec 3 SW ¼ of NW ¼........ 67
Twp 11 Sec 21 SW ¼ of SE ¼....... 56

Lyman, Amasa
Twp 11 Sec 19 NE ¼ of NE ¼...... 56

Lynch, Patrick
Twp 8 Sec 31 SE ¼ of SE ¼.......... 58

Lyon, Aaron C.
Twp 8 Sec 23 NE ¼ of SE ¼......... 59
Twp 8 Sec 23 SE ¼ of SE ¼.......... 59
Twp 8 Sec 24 SE ¼ of NW ¼....... 59
Twp 8 Sec 24 NE ¼ of SW ¼....... 59
Twp 8 Sec 24 SW ¼ of SW ¼....... 59
Twp 8 Sec 26 NE ¼ of NE ¼........ 59

Lyon, Carlos W.
Twp 8 Sec 24 NW ¼ of SW ¼...... 59

Lyon, Windsor P.
Twp 8 Sec 26 SW ¼ of SW ¼....... 59

Lyons, Caleb W.
Twp 9 Sec 32 SW ¼ of NW ¼....... 42

Lyons, John
Twp 9 Sec 32 SE ¼ of NW ¼........ 42

Lytle, John
Twp 12 Sec 36 NE ¼ of SE ¼....... 41
Twp 12 Sec 36 SE ¼ of SE ¼........ 41

Mackare, Jesse
Twp 8 Sec 31 SW ¼ of SW ¼........ 58

Mackley, Jeremiah
Twp 12 Sec 36 NW ¼ of SE ¼...... 41
Twp 12 Sec 36 SW ¼ of SE ¼....... 41

Mann, Jesse M.

Twp 7 Sec 7 NE ¼ of SW ¼........... 66
Twp 7 Sec 7 SE ¼ of SW ¼........... 66
Twp 7 Sec 18 NW ¼ of NE ¼....... 66
Twp 7 Sec 18 SW ¼ of NE ¼........ 66
Twp 7 Sec 18 SE ¼ of NE ¼......... 66
Twp 7 Sec 18 SW ¼ of SE ¼......... 66
Twp 8 Sec 22 NW ¼ of SE ¼........ 59
Twp 8 Sec 22 SW ¼ of SE ¼........ 59

Mark, John

Twp 7 Sec 35 NW ¼ of NE ¼....... 75
Twp 7 Sec 35 SW ¼ of NE ¼........ 75

Markwell, William

Twp 10 Sec 6 SW ¼ of NW ¼....... 64

Marsh, Nathan

Twp 9 Sec 4 NW ¼ of NW ¼........ 34
Twp 9 Sec 4 SW ¼ of NW ¼......... 34

Marsh, Thomas B.

Twp 11 Sec 2 NW ¼ of SW ¼....... 49
Twp 11 Sec 10 NW ¼ of NE ¼....... 49
Twp 11 Sec 10 SW ¼ of NE ¼...... 49
Twp 11 Sec 11 NE ¼ of NE ¼....... 49
Twp 11 Sec 11 NE ¼ of SE ¼....... 49
Twp 11 Sec 11 SE ¼ of SE ¼........ 49
Twp 12 Sec 35 SE ¼ of SE ¼........ 41

Martin, Moses

Twp 11 Sec 27 SW ¼ of SE ¼....... 57

Massingill, Samuel

Twp 8 Sec 26 NE ¼ of NW ¼....... 59

Maupin, Thomas

Twp 3 Sec 12 SE ¼ of SE ¼........... 39

Maynard, Jotham

Twp 8 Sec 32 NW ¼ of NW ¼...... 58
Twp 10 Sec 13 SW ¼ of NE ¼...... 65
Twp 11 Sec 2 NW ¼ of NW ¼....... 49
Twp 11 Sec 2 NE ¼ of NW ¼....... 49
Twp 11 Sec 2 SW ¼ of NW ¼....... 49
Twp 11 Sec 2 SE ¼ of NW ¼........ 49

McBee, David

Twp 1 Sec 22 SE ¼ of NW ¼........ 79
Twp 1 Sec 22 NW ¼ of SW ¼....... 79

McBee, James

Twp 1 Sec 23 NW ¼ of SW ¼....... 79
Twp 1 Sec 23 SW ¼ of SW ¼........ 79
Twp 10 Sec 24 NE ¼ of NW ¼..... 73

McBride, Thomas

Twp 2 Sec 9 SE ¼ of SW ¼........... 54
Twp 5 Sec 11 SW ¼ of SE ¼......... 53

McCarroll, Jesse

Twp 10 Sec 14 NW ¼ of NE ¼..... 65

McCord, James

Twp 10 Sec 12 NE ¼ of NW ¼..... 65

McCord, James B.

Twp 10 Sec 12 SE ¼ of NW ¼...... 65
Twp 11 Sec 30 SW ¼ of SE ¼....... 56

McDaniel, John Jr.

Twp 12 Sec 21 NE ¼ of SE ¼....... 40
Twp 12 Sec 21 SE ¼ of SE ¼........ 40

McDaniel, John Sen.

Twp 12 Sec 28 NE ¼ of NE ¼...... 40
Twp 12 Sec 28 SE ¼ of NE ¼...... 40

McDaniel, William G.

Twp 12 Sec 18 NW ¼ of SW ¼..... 32
Twp 12 Sec 18 SW ¼ of SW ¼...... 32
Twp 12 Sec 19 NW ¼ of NW ¼.... 40

McDonald, Jeremiah

Twp 10 Sec 27 SE ¼ of SW ¼....... 73
Twp 10 Sec 34 NW ¼ of NE ¼..... 73
Twp 10 Sec 34 SW ¼ of NE ¼...... 73
Twp 10 Sec 35 NW ¼ of SW ¼..... 73
Twp 10 Sec 35 SW ¼ of SW ¼...... 73

McDonald, Randolph

Twp 7 Sec 35 NE ¼ of NW ¼....... 75
Twp 7 Sec 35 SE ¼ of NW ¼....... 75
Twp 7 Sec 35 NW ¼ of SW ¼....... 75
Twp 7 Sec 35 NE ¼ of SW ¼....... 75
Twp 7 Sec 35 SE ¼ of SW ¼........ 75
Twp 10 Sec 35 SE ¼ of NW ¼..... 73

McDonald, Samual

Twp 10 Sec 35 NW ¼ of SW ¼..... 73
Twp 10 Sec 35 SW ¼ of SW ¼...... 73

McFee, Wallace

Twp 8 Sec 26 SE ¼ of NE ¼......... 59

McGee, James

Twp 10 Sec 24 NE ¼ of NW ¼..... 73

McGee, Samuel K.

Twp 10 Sec 21 NE ¼ of SW ¼...... 72
Twp 10 Sec 21 SE ¼ of SW ¼....... 72
Twp 10 Sec 27 NE ¼ of SW ¼...... 73
Twp 10 Sec 27 NW ¼ of SE ¼...... 73
Twp 10 Sec 27 SW ¼ of SE ¼....... 73
Twp 10 Sec 28 NE ¼ of NW ¼..... 72
Twp 10 Sec 28 NW ¼ of NE ¼..... 72
Twp 10 Sec 28 SE ¼ of NW ¼...... 72
Twp 10 Sec 28 SW ¼ of NE ¼...... 72
Twp 10 Sec 28 SE ¼ of NE ¼....... 72
Twp 10 Sec 34 NE ¼ of NW ¼..... 73
Twp 10 Sec 34 NE ¼ of NE ¼...... 73
Twp 10 Sec 34 SE ¼ of NW ¼...... 73
Twp 10 Sec 34 SE ¼ of NE ¼....... 73
Twp 10 Sec 34 NW ¼ of SE ¼...... 73
Twp 10 Sec 34 NE ¼ of SE ¼....... 73
Twp 10 Sec 34 SW ¼ of SE ¼....... 73
Twp 10 Sec 34 SE ¼ of SE ¼........ 73

McGuire, Francis

Twp 8 Sec 26 NW ¼ of NW ¼...... 59

McHenry, Henry

Twp 8 Sec 26 SW ¼ of NW ¼....... 59
Twp 8 Sec 26 SW ¼ of SE ¼....... 59
Twp 8 Sec 35 NW ¼ of NE ¼...... 59
Twp 8 Sec 35 NE ¼ of NE ¼....... 59
Twp 8 Sec 35 SE ¼ of NE ¼........ 59
Twp 8 Sec 36 NW ¼ of NW ¼..... 59

McHenry, Henry

Twp 8 Sec 22 NE ¼ of SE ¼......... 59

McKissick, Wilson

Twp 11 Sec 20 SE ¼ of NE ¼....... 56

McKown, Marcellus

Twp 10 Sec 14 SE ¼ of SE ¼........ 65

McLellen, William E.

Twp 11 Sec 8 SE ¼ of SW ¼......... 48

Merrill, Gilman

Twp 2 Sec 3 NW ¼ of SE ¼.......... 55
Twp 2 Sec 3 SW ¼ of SE ¼.......... 55

Merrill, Gilmon

Twp 2 Sec 7 SW ¼ of SE ¼........... 54
Twp 2 Sec 17 NW ¼ of NW ¼...... 54

Merrill, Thomas

Twp 2 Sec 3 SE ¼ of NW ¼.......... 55
Twp 2 Sec 18 NE ¼ of NE ¼........ 54
Twp 2 Sec 18 SE ¼ of NE ¼......... 54

Middaugh, Benjamin

Twp 11 Sec 32 SE ¼ of NE ¼....... 56
Twp 12 Sec 18 NW ¼ of SE ¼...... 32

Middleton, Reuben

Twp 5 Sec 19 NW ¼ of SE ¼........ 60
Twp 5 Sec 19 SW ¼ of SE ¼......... 60

Middleton, William

Twp 5 Sec 19 NE ¼ of SE ¼......... 60

Miles, Daniel S.

Twp 7 Sec 35 SW ¼ of SW ¼........ 75

Miles, Samuel

Twp 11 Sec 17 NE ¼ of NE ¼...... 48
Twp 11 Sec 24 NW ¼ of SW ¼..... 57
Twp 11 Sec 24 SW ¼ of SW ¼...... 57
Twp 11 Sec 25 NE ¼ of NW ¼..... 57

Miller, Abraham

Twp 8 Sec 26 SE ¼ of NW ¼........ 59

Miller, Charles A.

Twp 5 Sec 2 NW ¼ of NW ¼........ 53
Twp 5 Sec 2 SW ¼ of NW ¼......... 53

Miller, Eleazur

Twp 8 Sec 15 NE ¼ of SE ¼......... 51
Twp 8 Sec 23 SW ¼ of SW ¼........ 59

Miller, George

Twp 2 Sec 7 NE ¼ of SE ¼........... 54

Twp 12 Sec 18 SW ¼ of NW ¼..... 32
Twp 12 Sec 18 NE ¼ of SW ¼...... 32
Twp 12 Sec 18 SE ¼ of SW ¼....... 32

Parmer, Ambrse
Twp 11 Sec 26 NW ¼ of NW ¼.... 57
Twp 11 Sec 26 SW ¼ of NW ¼..... 57

Parrman, Giles
Twp 3 Sec 1 NW ¼ of SE ¼.......... 39
Twp 3 Sec 1 NE ¼ of SE ¼........... 39
Twp 3 Sec 1 SW ¼ of SE ¼........... 39
Twp 3 Sec 1 SE ¼ of SE ¼........... 39

Parsons, Thorit
Twp 10 Sec 24 SE ¼ of SW ¼....... 73

Partridge, Edward
Twp 11 Sec 5 NW ¼ of SW ¼....... 48
Twp 11 Sec 5 SW ¼ of SW ¼........ 48
Twp 11 Sec 12 NE ¼ of NW ¼..... 49
Twp 11 Sec 12 SE ¼ of NW ¼...... 49
Twp 11 Sec 20 SE ¼ of NW ¼...... 56
Twp 11 Sec 22 NW ¼ of NW ¼..... 57
Twp 11 Sec 29 NE ¼ of NW ¼...... 56
Twp 11 Sec 29 NW ¼ of NE ¼..... 56
Twp 11 Sec 29 SW ¼ of NE ¼...... 56

Patten, Charles W.
Twp 11 Sec 6 NW ¼ of NW ¼...... 48
Twp 12 Sec 31 SE ¼ of SW ¼....... 40

Patten, John
Twp 11 Sec 4 NW ¼ of NW ¼...... 48
Twp 11 Sec 5 NW ¼ of NE ¼...... 48
Twp 11 Sec 5 NE ¼ of NE ¼........ 48
Twp 12 Sec 18 NE ¼ of NW ¼..... 32
Twp 12 Sec 18 SE ¼ of NW ¼...... 32
Twp 12 Sec 33 SW ¼ of SW ¼...... 40

Patten, William W.
Twp 12 Sec 29 NE ¼ of NW ¼..... 40
Twp 12 Sec 32 SE ¼ of SE ¼........ 40

Patton, Charles
Twp 9 Sec 35 NW ¼ of NE ¼....... 43
Twp 9 Sec 35 SW ¼ of NE ¼........ 43

Pea, John
Twp 9 Sec 30 NW ¼ of NW ¼...... 42
Twp 12 Sec 25 SE ¼ of NE ¼....... 41

Peck, Joseph
Twp 12 Sec 23 SW ¼ of NE ¼...... 41

Peck, Reed
Twp 11 Sec 27 SE ¼ of NE ¼....... 57

Phelps, Morris
Twp 11 Sec 26 SE ¼ of NE ¼....... 57
Twp 11 Sec 26 NE ¼ of SE ¼....... 57

Phelps, Orrin
Twp 11 Sec 26 NE ¼ of NE ¼...... 57
Twp 11 Sec 26 SW ¼ of NE ¼...... 57

Phelps, William W.
Twp 11 Sec 1 NE ¼ of NE ¼........ 49
Twp 11 Sec 1 SE ¼ of NE ¼........ 49
Twp 11 Sec 8 NE ¼ of SE ¼........ 48
Twp 11 Sec 9 NW ¼ of SW ¼....... 48
Twp 11 Sec 9 NE ¼ of SE ¼........ 48
Twp 11 Sec 9 SW ¼ of SW ¼....... 48
Twp 11 Sec 9 SE ¼ of SE ¼.......... 48
Twp 11 Sec 10 NE ¼ of SW ¼...... 49
Twp 11 Sec 10 NW ¼ of SE ¼...... 49
Twp 11 Sec 10 NE ¼ of SE ¼....... 49
Twp 11 Sec 10 SE ¼ of SW ¼....... 49
Twp 11 Sec 10 SW ¼ of SE ¼....... 49
Twp 11 Sec 10 SE ¼ of SE ¼........ 49
Twp 11 Sec 11 NE ¼ of NW ¼..... 49
Twp 11 Sec 11 SE ¼ of NW ¼...... 49
Twp 11 Sec 11 NW ¼ of SW ¼..... 49
Twp 11 Sec 11 NE ¼ of SW ¼...... 49
Twp 11 Sec 11 NW ¼ of SE ¼...... 49
Twp 11 Sec 11 SW ¼ of SW ¼...... 49
Twp 11 Sec 11 SE ¼ of SW ¼....... 49
Twp 11 Sec 11 SW ¼ of SE ¼....... 49
Twp 11 Sec 15 NE ¼ of SE ¼....... 49
Twp 11 Sec 15 SE ¼ of SE ¼........ 49
Twp 12 Sec 33 NE ¼ of NE ¼...... 40
Twp 12 Sec 33 SE ¼ of NE ¼....... 40
Twp 12 Sec 35 NW ¼ of SE ¼...... 41
Twp 12 Sec 35 SW ¼ of SE ¼....... 41

Piburn, Joseph
Twp 7 Sec 20 NE ¼ of NW ¼....... 74

Plumb, Merlin
Twp 1 Sec 8 SW ¼ of NW ¼......... 70
Twp 1 Sec 8 NW ¼ of SW ¼......... 70
Twp 1 Sec 8 NE ¼ of SW ¼......... 70
Twp 1 Sec 8 SE ¼ of SW ¼.......... 70

Pobler, Zilpha
Twp 10 Sec 33 SE ¼ of NE ¼....... 72

Potter, Thomas
Twp 10 Sec 32 SE ¼ of SW ¼....... 72
Twp 10 Sec 32 SW ¼ of SE ¼....... 72

Potts, Jacob H.
Twp 2 Sec 13 NW ¼ of SE ¼........ 55
Twp 2 Sec 13 SW ¼ of SE ¼......... 55

Powell, Uriah B.
Twp 11 Sec 11 SE ¼ of NE ¼....... 49
Twp 12 Sec 35 NE ¼ of SE ¼....... 41

Prindle, James O.
Twp 11 Sec 31 NW ¼ of SE ¼..... 56

Prindle, Roswell
Twp 11 Sec 31 NE ¼ of SW ¼...... 56
Twp 11 Sec 31 SW ¼ of SW ¼...... 56
Twp 11 Sec 31 SE ¼ of SW ¼....... 56
Twp 11 Sec 31 SW ¼ of SE ¼....... 56

Pye, William H.
Twp 5 Sec 15 NW ¼ of NE ¼....... 53
Twp 5 Sec 15 SW ¼ of NW ¼....... 53
Twp 5 Sec 15 SE ¼ of NW ¼........ 53
Twp 5 Sec 15 SW ¼ of NE ¼........ 53

Pyler, Jonathan
Twp 8 Sec 28 SW ¼ of NE ¼....... 58

Raglin, John
Twp 8 Sec 25 NW ¼ of NW ¼...... 59
Twp 8 Sec 25 NE ¼ of NW ¼...... 59
Twp 8 Sec 25 SW ¼ of NW ¼...... 59
Twp 8 Sec 25 SE ¼ of NW ¼........ 59

Ramsey, James M.
Twp 8 Sec 28 NW ¼ of NE ¼...... 58
Twp 8 Sec 28 NE ¼ of NE ¼........ 58

Randall, Miles
Twp 11 Sec 30 NE ¼ of NE ¼...... 56

Randle, Miles
Twp 11 Sec 21 SW ¼ of SW ¼...... 56

Rathbun, Hiram
Twp 5 Sec 2 NW ¼ of NE ¼......... 53
Twp 6 Sec 25 NE ¼ of SW ¼....... 45

Rathbun, Robert
Twp 2 Sec 9 SE ¼ of SE ¼............ 54
Twp 6 Sec 35 NE ¼ of NE ¼....... 45
Twp 6 Sec 35 NW ¼ of SE ¼....... 45
Twp 6 Sec 35 SW ¼ of SE ¼........ 45

Redford, John
Twp 11 Sec 36 SE ¼ of NW ¼...... 57

Reed, Elijah
Twp 8 Sec 32 SW ¼ of NW ¼....... 58

Reynolds, John
Twp 1 Sec 6 SW ¼ of SE ¼........... 70
Twp 1 Sec 7 NW ¼ of NE ¼......... 70
Twp 1 Sec 7 SW ¼ of NE ¼......... 70
Twp 10 Sec 35 NW ¼ of NW ¼.... 73
Twp 10 Sec 35 SW ¼ of NW ¼..... 73

Reynolds, Stephen W.
Twp 3 Sec 12 NE ¼ of SE ¼......... 39

Rich, Charles C. & Joseph
Twp 10 Sec 3 NW ¼ of NE ¼....... 65
Twp 10 Sec 3 SW ¼ of NW ¼...... 65
Twp 10 Sec 3 SE ¼ of NW ¼........ 65
Twp 10 Sec 3 SW ¼ of NE ¼........ 65
Twp 11 Sec 33 SW ¼ of SE ¼....... 56

Rich, Landon
Twp 10 Sec 15 NE ¼ of NE ¼...... 65
Twp 10 Sec 15 SW ¼ of NE ¼...... 65
Twp 10 Sec 15 SE ¼ of NE ¼........ 65

Richardson, James
Twp 12 Sec 34 NW ¼ of NE ¼..... 41

Richardson, John C.
Twp 7 Sec 4 SE ¼ of NE ¼............ 66

Richardson, Josiah
Twp 5 Sec 19 NW ¼ of NE ¼....... 60

Riggs, Burr
Twp 8 Sec 22 SE ¼ of NW ¼........ 59
Twp 11 Sec 11 NW ¼ of NW ¼..... 49
Twp 11 Sec 14 NE ¼ of SW ¼...... 49
Twp 11 Sec 14 SE ¼ of SW ¼....... 49
Twp 11 Sec 20 NW ¼ of NE ¼..... 56
Twp 12 Sec 28 SE ¼ of SW ¼....... 40

Ripley, Alansen
Twp 10 Sec 28 SW ¼ of SE ¼....... 72

Ripley, Alanson
Twp 11 Sec 10 SE ¼ of NW ¼...... 49
Twp 11 Sec 17 SW ¼ of NE ¼..... 48
Twp 11 Sec 17 SW ¼ of SE ¼....... 48

Rockhold, Asa
Twp 8 Sec 23 NW ¼ of NE ¼....... 59
Twp 8 Sec 23 SW ¼ of NE ¼....... 59

Rockhold, Loyd
Twp 3 Sec 2 SE ¼ of SW ¼............ 39

Rockwell, Orren
Twp 7 Sec 5 NW ¼ of SW ¼......... 66
Twp 7 Sec 6 NE ¼ of SE ¼............ 66

Rockwell, Porter
Twp 11 Sec 26 NW ¼ of NE ¼..... 57

Rogers, Samuel
Twp 8 Sec 12 NW ¼ of SW ¼....... 51
Twp 8 Sec 12 NE ¼ of SW ¼........ 51
Twp 8 Sec 12 SW ¼ of SW ¼........ 51

Rolfe, Samuel
Twp 11 Sec 4 SW ¼ of SE ¼......... 48

Rollins, James H.
Twp 11 Sec 13 NW ¼ of SE ¼...... 49

Rose, Andrew
Twp 8 Sec 28 NW ¼ of SE ¼........ 58
Twp 8 Sec 28 SE ¼ of SW ¼.......... 58
Twp 8 Sec 28 SE ¼ of SE ¼.......... 58
Twp 8 Sec 33 NE ¼ of NW ¼........ 58
Twp 8 Sec 33 NW ¼ of NE ¼........ 58
Twp 8 Sec 33 SE ¼ of NW ¼........ 58

Rowland, John
Twp 8 Sec 27 NW ¼ of NE ¼....... 59
Twp 8 Sec 27 SW ¼ of NE ¼........ 59

Rowley, John
Twp 8 Sec 29 SW ¼ of SE ¼.......... 58
Twp 8 Sec 29 SE ¼ of SE ¼........... 58

Saley, James Jr.
Twp 8 Sec 17 NW ¼ of SE ¼......... 50

Salisbury, Joshua
Twp 2 Sec 19 NE ¼ of NW ¼....... 62

Sanders, Moses M.
Twp 11 Sec 30 SW ¼ of SW ¼..... 56

Sargent, Abel M.
Twp 11 Sec 3 SE ¼ of NE ¼......... 49
Twp 11 Sec 10 SW ¼ of SW ¼...... 49

Sayers, John
Twp 11 Sec 34 NW ¼ of NE ¼..... 57

Scovel, Abner
Twp 11 Sec 36 NE ¼ of NW ¼..... 57
Twp 11 Sec 36 NW ¼ of SE ¼...... 57
Twp 11 Sec 36 NE ¼ of SE ¼....... 57

Scrichfield, Absalom
Twp 10 Sec 4 NW ¼ of NW ¼...... 64

Selvey, Walter
Twp 10 Sec 13 NW ¼ of SE ¼...... 65

Selvy, Walter
Twp 10 Sec 14 NW ¼ of SW ¼..... 65
Twp 10 Sec 14 NE ¼ of SW ¼...... 65

Severe, James
Twp 2 Sec 3 SW ¼ of NE ¼.......... 55

Shaw, Elijah
Twp 5 Sec 21 SW ¼ of NW ¼....... 60
Twp 5 Sec 21 NW ¼ of SW ¼....... 60

Shearer, Daniel
Twp 8 Sec 31 NE ¼ of SE ¼......... 58
Twp 11 Sec 23 NE ¼ of NW ¼.... 57
Twp 11 Sec 23 SE ¼ of NW ¼..... 57

Shearer, Joel
Twp 8 Sec 15 NE ¼ of SW ¼....... 51
Twp 8 Sec 15 SE ¼ of SW ¼........ 51
Twp 8 Sec 22 NW ¼ of NE ¼....... 59
Twp 11 Sec 22 NW ¼ of NE ¼.... 57
Twp 11 Sec 22 SW ¼ of NE ¼..... 57
Twp 11 Sec 22 SE ¼ of NE ¼...... 57

Shepherd, Samuel
Twp 12 Sec 9 NW ¼ of SE ¼....... 32
Twp 12 Sec 35 NE ¼ of NW ¼.... 41
Twp 12 Sec 35 SE ¼ of NW ¼..... 41

Sherman, Almon
Twp 11 Sec 17 NW ¼ of NE ¼..... 48

Sherman, Gardner
Twp 10 Sec 2 SW ¼ of SE ¼......... 65

Skidmore, John
Twp 7 Sec 17 NW ¼ of NE ¼....... 66
Twp 7 Sec 17 SE ¼ of NW ¼........ 66

Skidmore, Thomas
Twp 7 Sec 17 SW ¼ of NE ¼........ 66

Slade, Benjamin
Twp 11 Sec 36 SW ¼ of SE ¼....... 57
Twp 11 Sec 36 SE ¼ of SE ¼........ 57

Slade, George
Twp 10 Sec 11 NW ¼ of SE ¼...... 65

Sloan, Albert
Twp 11 Sec 30 SE ¼ of SE ¼........ 56

Smith, Avery
Twp 7 Sec 6 NW ¼ of NW ¼........ 66
Twp 8 Sec 31 NW ¼ of SW ¼....... 58

Smith, Hiram
Twp 10 Sec 12 NW ¼ of NE ¼..... 65
Twp 10 Sec 12 SW ¼ of NE ¼..... 65
Twp 10 Sec 12 SW ¼ of SW ¼..... 65
Twp 11 Sec 1 NW ¼ of SW ¼...... 49
Twp 11 Sec 1 NE ¼ of SW ¼....... 49
Twp 11 Sec 1 NW ¼ of SE ¼....... 49
Twp 11 Sec 1 SW ¼ of SW ¼...... 49
Twp 11 Sec 1 SE ¼ of SW ¼......... 49
Twp 11 Sec 1 SW ¼ of SE ¼......... 49
Twp 11 Sec 2 NE ¼ of SW ¼........ 49
Twp 11 Sec 2 SE ¼ of SW ¼......... 49
Twp 11 Sec 12 NW ¼ of NW ¼.... 49
Twp 11 Sec 12 SW ¼ of NW ¼..... 49
Twp 11 Sec 12 NW ¼ of SW ¼..... 49
Twp 11 Sec 12 SW ¼ of SW ¼..... 49
Twp 12 Sec 28 NW ¼ of SE ¼...... 40
Twp 12 Sec 28 SW ¼ of SE ¼...... 40
Twp 12 Sec 33 NW ¼ of NE ¼..... 40
Twp 12 Sec 33 SW ¼ of NE ¼...... 40

Smith, Jesse
Twp 10 Sec 28 NW ¼ of NW ¼.... 72

Smith, Joseph Jr.
Twp 11 Sec 2 NE ¼ of NE ¼........ 49
Twp 11 Sec 2 SE ¼ of NE ¼......... 49
Twp 11 Sec 22 NW ¼ of SE ¼...... 57
Twp 11 Sec 22 SW ¼ of SE ¼....... 57
Twp 11 Sec 27 NW ¼ of NW ¼.... 57
Twp 11 Sec 27 NE ¼ of NW ¼..... 57
Twp 11 Sec 27 NW ¼ of NE ¼..... 57
Twp 11 Sec 27 SW ¼ of NW ¼..... 57
Twp 11 Sec 27 SE ¼ of NW ¼...... 57
Twp 11 Sec 27 SW ¼ of NE ¼...... 57
Twp 11 Sec 27 NW ¼ of SW ¼..... 57
Twp 11 Sec 27 NE ¼ of SW ¼...... 57
Twp 11 Sec 27 SW ¼ of SW ¼..... 57
Twp 11 Sec 27 SE ¼ of SW ¼....... 57

Smith, Sardis
Twp 2 Sec 7 NE ¼ of SW ¼.......... 54
Twp 3 Sec 32 NE ¼ of SE ¼......... 46

Smith, William
Twp 11 Sec 10 NW ¼ of NW ¼.... 49
Twp 11 Sec 10 SW ¼ of NW ¼..... 49

Turner, Cornelius B.

Twp 5 Sec 9 SE ¼ of NE ¼......... 52

Turner, Lewis

Twp 10 Sec 2 NE ¼ of SE ¼......... 65
Twp 10 Sec 2 SE ¼ of SE ¼.......... 65
Twp 10 Sec 11 NE ¼ of NE ¼...... 65

Turnidge, William

Twp 8 Sec 24 SE ¼ of SW ¼....... 59
Twp 8 Sec 24 SW ¼ of SE ¼....... 59
Twp 8 Sec 25 NW ¼ of NE ¼....... 59
Twp 8 Sec 25 SW ¼ of NE ¼........ 59

Turnidy, William

Twp 5 Sec 20 NW ¼ of NW ¼...... 60
Twp 5 Sec 20 SW ¼ of NW ¼....... 60

Tyrrel, Oliver H.

Twp 3 Sec 14 SE ¼ of SW ¼......... 39
Twp 3 Sec 23 NW ¼ of NE ¼....... 47

Vanderliss, Wilson

Twp 8 Sec 32 NE ¼ of SE ¼....... 58

Venable, Hugh

Twp 12 Sec 32 NW ¼ of NE ¼..... 40
Twp 12 Sec 32 SW ¼ of NE ¼...... 40

Vorhees, Elisha

Twp 10 Sec 10 NE ¼ of NW ¼..... 65

Walker, James

Twp 7 Sec 8 SE ¼ of NE ¼........... 66

Walker, Oliver

Twp 2 Sec 1 NE ¼ of SE ¼.......... 55
Twp 2 Sec 1 SE ¼ of SE ¼........... 55
Twp 2 Sec 12 NE ¼ of NE ¼....... 55
Twp 2 Sec 12 SW ¼ of NE ¼....... 55
Twp 2 Sec 12 SE ¼ of NE ¼....... 55
Twp 2 Sec 12 NW ¼ of SE ¼....... 55
Twp 2 Sec 12 NE ¼ of SE ¼....... 55
Twp 2 Sec 12 SE ¼ of SE ¼....... 55

Walter, George

Twp 10 Sec 12 NE ¼ of SE ¼....... 65
Twp 10 Sec 12 SE ¼ of SE ¼....... 65
Twp 11 Sec 12 NE ¼ of NE ¼...... 49
Twp 11 Sec 12 SE ¼ of NE ¼...... 49
Twp 11 Sec 13 NW ¼ of NE ¼..... 49
Twp 11 Sec 13 NE ¼ of NE ¼...... 49
Twp 11 Sec 13 SW ¼ of NE ¼...... 49
Twp 11 Sec 13 SE ¼ of NE ¼...... 49
Twp 11 Sec 36 NW ¼ of NW ¼..... 57
Twp 11 Sec 36 SW ¼ of NW ¼..... 57

Walton, Richard

Twp 6 Sec 28 NW ¼ of SW ¼....... 44
Twp 6 Sec 28 SW ¼ of SW ¼........ 44
Twp 6 Sec 33 NW ¼ of NW ¼....... 44

Warner, Lorenzo

Twp 2 Sec 7 SE ¼ of SE ¼............ 54
Twp 3 Sec 33 SE ¼ of SE ¼......... 46

Twp 5 Sec 2 NE ¼ of NE ¼....... 53
Twp 6 Sec 35 NW ¼ of SW ¼....... 45
Twp 6 Sec 35 NE ¼ of SW ¼....... 45
Twp 6 Sec 35 SW ¼ of SW ¼....... 45
Twp 6 Sec 35 SE ¼ of SW ¼......... 45

Weaver, Edward

Twp 8 Sec 30 SE ¼ of SE ¼.......... 58

Wheeler, John

Twp 8 Sec 26 NW ¼ of NE ¼....... 59
Twp 8 Sec 26 SW ¼ of NE ¼........ 59

Whitaker, Samuel

Twp 10 Sec 32 SW ¼ of NE ¼...... 72
Twp 10 Sec 32 NW ¼ of SE ¼...... 72

White, Robert

Twp 2 Sec 9 NW ¼ of SW ¼......... 54
Twp 2 Sec 9 NE ¼ of SW ¼......... 54
Twp 2 Sec 9 NW ¼ of SE ¼......... 54
Twp 2 Sec 9 SW ¼ of SW ¼......... 54
Twp 2 Sec 17 SW ¼ of NW ¼....... 54
Twp 2 Sec 18 SE ¼ of SW ¼......... 54

Whiteside, Alexander

Twp 11 Sec 2 SW ¼ of SW ¼....... 49

Whiting, Charles

Twp 10 Sec 6 NE ¼ of SE ¼......... 64

Whiting, Edwin

Twp 10 Sec 5 NE ¼ of NE ¼......... 64
Twp 10 Sec 5 SE ¼ of NE ¼......... 64

Whiting, Elisha

Twp 10 Sec 5 NW ¼ of NE ¼....... 64
Twp 10 Sec 5 SW ¼ of NE ¼........ 64

Whitlock, Andrew

Twp 10 Sec 12 NW ¼ of NW ¼.... 65

Whitlock, Austin

Twp 10 Sec 2 NW ¼ of NE ¼....... 65
Twp 10 Sec 2 SW ¼ of NE ¼........ 65

Whitmer, David

Twp 8 Sec 7 SE ¼ of SW ¼........... 50

Whitmer, Jacob

Twp 11 Sec 3 SW ¼ of NW ¼....... 49
Twp 11 Sec 8 SE ¼ of SE ¼.......... 48
Twp 12 Sec 34 NW ¼ of SW ¼..... 41

Whitmer, John

Twp 8 Sec 17 SW ¼ of NW ¼....... 50
Twp 11 Sec 3 NW ¼ of NE ¼....... 49
Twp 11 Sec 3 SW ¼ of NE ¼........ 49
Twp 11 Sec 14 NW ¼ of NW ¼.... 49
Twp 11 Sec 14 NE ¼ of NW ¼..... 49
Twp 11 Sec 14 NW ¼ of NE ¼..... 49
Twp 11 Sec 14 SW ¼ of NW ¼..... 49
Twp 11 Sec 14 SE ¼ of NW ¼...... 49
Twp 11 Sec 14 SW ¼ of NE ¼...... 49
Twp 11 Sec 14 NW ¼ of SW ¼..... 49
Twp 11 Sec 14 NW ¼ of SE ¼...... 49

Twp 11 Sec 14 NE ¼ of SE ¼....... 49
Twp 11 Sec 14 SW ¼ of SW ¼...... 49
Twp 11 Sec 14 SW ¼ of SE ¼...... 49
Twp 11 Sec 15 NE ¼ of NW ¼..... 49
Twp 11 Sec 15 NW ¼ of NE ¼..... 49
Twp 11 Sec 15 NE ¼ of NE ¼...... 49
Twp 11 Sec 15 SE ¼ of NW ¼...... 49
Twp 11 Sec 15 SW ¼ of NE ¼...... 49
Twp 11 Sec 15 SE ¼ of NE ¼....... 49
Twp 11 Sec 15 NW ¼ of SE ¼...... 49
Twp 11 Sec 15 SW ¼ of SE ¼....... 49
Twp 11 Sec 22 NW ¼ of NW ¼.... 57
Twp 11 Sec 22 SW ¼ of NW ¼..... 57
Twp 11 Sec 23 NW ¼ of NW ¼.... 57
Twp 11 Sec 23 SW ¼ of NW ¼..... 57
Twp 12 Sec 35 NE ¼ of NE ¼...... 41
Twp 12 Sec 35 SE ¼ of NE ¼....... 41

Wight, Lyman

Twp 11 Sec 34 NE ¼ of NE ¼...... 57

Wightman, Charles

Twp 8 Sec 19 SE ¼ of SE ¼.......... 58

Wightman, William

Twp 8 Sec 19 SW ¼ of SE ¼......... 58
Twp 8 Sec 30 SE ¼ of NE ¼......... 58

William, George

Twp 6 Sec 25 SW ¼ of NW ¼....... 45

Williams, Alexander

Twp 5 Sec 12 NW ¼ of SE ¼........ 53

Williams, Frederick G.

Twp 8 Sec 7 NW ¼ of SW ¼......... 50

Williams, George

Twp 6 Sec 25 NW ¼ of SW ¼....... 45
Twp 6 Sec 25 SW ¼ of SW ¼........ 45
Twp 6 Sec 25 SE ¼ of SW ¼......... 45

Willis, William M.

Twp 5 Sec 12 SE ¼ of SW ¼......... 53

Wilson, Eli

Twp 3 Sec 2 NW ¼ of SW ¼......... 39
Twp 3 Sec 2 SW ¼ of SW ¼......... 39

Wilson, Henry H.

Twp 2 Sec 3 SE ¼ of SE ¼............ 55

Wilson, Lewis D.

Twp 1 Sec 14 NE ¼ of SW ¼........ 71
Twp 1 Sec 14 NW ¼ of SE ¼........ 71
Twp 1 Sec 14 NE ¼ of SE ¼......... 71
Twp 1 Sec 14 SE ¼ of SW ¼......... 71
Twp 1 Sec 14 SW ¼ of SE ¼......... 71
Twp 1 Sec 14 SE ¼ of SE ¼.......... 71

Wilson, Whitford G.

Twp 1 Sec 23 NE ¼ of NW ¼....... 79
Twp 1 Sec 26 NW ¼ of NW ¼...... 79
Twp 1 Sec 26 SW ¼ of NW ¼....... 79

Bibliography

SCRIPTURAL REFERENCES

————, *A Book of Commandments for the Government of the Church of Christ*, Zion [Independence]: W.W. Phelps & Co., 1833, facsimile reprinted by Wilford C. Wood in *Joseph Smith Begins His Work* (v. ii), Salt Lake City: Melchizedek Priesthood Properties, Inc., 1995.

Smith, Joseph Jr., Oliver Cowdery, Sidney Rigdon and Frederick G. Williams, (eds.), *Doctrine and Covenants of the Church of the Latter Day Saints*, Kirtland: F.G. Williams & Co., 1835, facsimile reprinted by Wilford C. Wood in *Joseph Smith Begins His Work* (v. ii), Salt Lake City: Melchizedek Priesthood Properties, Inc., 1995.

————, *Book of Doctrine and Covenants*, Independence: Herald Publishing House, 2000.

————, *The Doctrine and Covenants of The Church of Jesus Christ of Latter-day Saints*, Salt Lake City: Intellectual Reserve, Inc., 2000.

WORKS CITED

Baugh, Alexander L., *A Call to Arms: The 1838 Mormon Defense of Northern Missouri*, Provo: Joseph Fielding Smith Institute and BYU Studies, 2000.

Berrett, Lamar C., general ed., and Max H. Perkin, ed., *Sacred Places: A Comprehensive Guide to Early LDS Historical Sites*, Vol. 4: Missouri, Salt Lake City: Deseret Book, 2004.

Brown, Kent S., Donald Q. Cannon and Richard H. Jackson, (eds.), *Historical Atlas of Mormonism*, New York: Simon & Schuster, 1994.

Garrett, Wilbur E., and John B. Garver, Jr., (eds.), *Historical Atlas of the United States*, Washington, D.C.: The National Geographic Society, 1993.

Johnson, Clark V. and Ronald E. Romig, *An Index to Early Caldwell County, Missouri Land Records*, Independence: Missouri Mormon Frontier Foundation, 2002.

Johnson, Clark V., *Mormon Redress Petitions: Documents of the 1833-38 Missouri Conflict*, Provo: Religious Studies Center, Brigham Young University, 1992.

Legg, Phillip R., *Oliver Cowdery: The Elusive Second Elder of the Restoration*, Independence: Herald Publishing House, 1989.

LeSueur, Stephen C., *The 1838 Mormon War in Missouri*, Columbia: University of Missouri Press, 1990.

Quinn, D. Michael, *The Mormon Hierarchy: Origins of Power*, Salt Lake City, Signature Books and Smith Research Assoc., 1994.

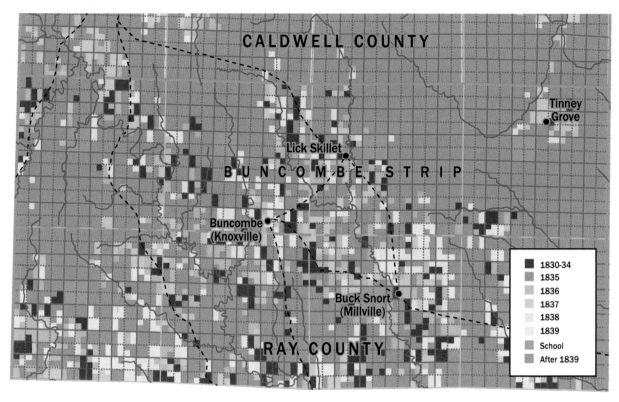

MAP 19: Land purchased in the Buncombe Strip by date. During the Mormon period, this strip was a non-county area attached to Ray County for judicial purposes. After the Mormon War, it was annexed to Ray County.

About the Author

JOHN C. HAMER is a map-maker and historian whose work focuses on the Latter Day Saint Movement. His maps have been published in dozens of books, journals, museum exhibits, and documentary films. He is co-author of *Community of Christ: An Illustrated History* and co-editor of *Scattering of the Saints: Schism within Mormonism*. From 2010–2011 he served as president of the John Whitmer Historical Association and he served as founding editor of John Whitmer Books from 2005–2011.

John is a great, great, great, great grandson of Stephen and Nancy Winchester — early Latter Day Saints who owned 120 acres of farmland in Caldwell County just east of present-day Mirabile (see map on page 57). John is an active member of the downtown Toronto, Ontario, congregation of the Community of Christ.

Made in the USA
Monee, IL
29 August 2022